THE BOOK OF TENNIS

The book of TENNIS

ow to play the game

BY THE EDITORS OF

WORLD TENNIS MAGAZINE

and CORNEL LUMIERE

With an introduction by

JACK KRAMER

Cartoons by

JEFF CHAPLEAU

Book Design: Howard Munce

by GLADYS HELDMAN
and CORNEL LUMIERE

Library of Congress Catalog Card Number: 64-21266
ISBN: 0-448-01948-5

Printed in the United States of America

WORLD TENNIS is a monthly
magazine published in
New York. Its editor is
Gladys Heldman. Cornel
Lumière, who has written
on tennis and other sports,
lives in Jamaica, W.I.

Grateful acknowledgment is made to
Ed Fernberger for assistance in
picture editing; the major portion
of the photographs in this book
were taken by him.

Some of the illustrations and text
originally appeared in
BETTER TENNIS WITH
THE WORLD'S BEST PLAYERS
by Cornel Lumière, published
by Eyre & Spottiswoode Ltd.
in England in 1963.

COVER:
Rod Laver
Photo by Ed Fernberger

PLAY TENNIS WITH A PLAN

takes time to become a good tennis player. It takes complete devotion to become a champion. Whatever the time and cost it is worth it: Tennis gives more than it takes.

Decide what you expect from this great game and what you are prepared to give to it. The pleasure of good tennis will last your lifetime. King Gustav of Sweden, "Mr. G." on the courts, played tournament tennis until the age of 84!

The demands the game makes on you are exacting—constant training and continuity of effort, fitness and mental alertness, great patience and good sportsmanship.

The world's greatest players have reached the top by way of superb physical conditioning. This takes planning and sacrifice. Look what stamina means in tennis: J. Drobny and J. E. Patty divided their singles match after four hours' play with a score of 1-19, 8-10, 21-21 in Lyons in 1955. Schroeder and Falkenburg beat Gonzalez and Stewart after 4¾ hours of play with a score of 36-34, 3-6, 4-6, 6-4, 19-17, or a total of 135 games in Los Angeles in 1949.

Watch good tennis. The wonderful anticipation and co-ordination, the grace and ease of champion players, their marvelous balance and control, these the young player can emulate only by building up his game.

Take the time to analyze tennis, every stroke. However easy it may look when you watch an experienced player, this is one of the most difficult sports. Know *why* and *how* to do what is right and avoid the superfluous. It's much easier to start out right than to have to correct at great cost of time incorrect motions and flaws you may have acquired through lack of knowledge and inattention to the tenets of technique. Good tennis comes of learning all about the game and then putting this knowledge into action. Even then there are so many factors beyond your control that every game you play will continue to be an exciting and unpredictable match of skills, circumstances and personalities.

My first 25 years in this sport have been more than good to me. May the game of tennis be more than good to you!

JACK KRAMER

CONTENTS

What Tennis Calls For

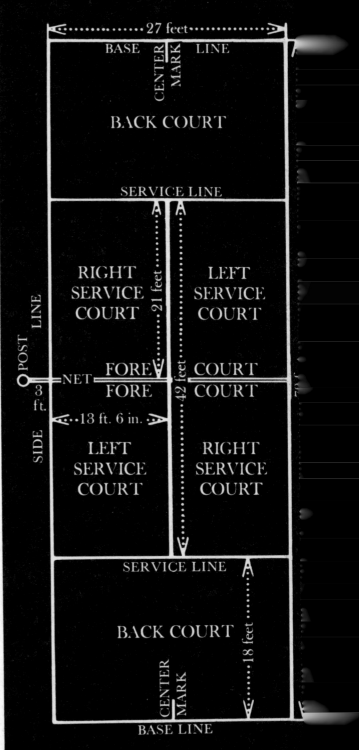

DIAGRAM AND DIMENSIONS OF SINGLES COURT

THE EQUIPMENT YOU NEED
The very best equipment you can afford is the minimum you should have.

THE RACKET
Rackets are made in three weights—light, medium and heavy. Buy a frame that seems relatively light to you. Select a brand name. A fairly light racket is much easier to handle than a racket that is too heavy. Time and experience will teach you the exact weight of racket that is best for you. This is true also of the thickness of the handle. Too thick a handle will result in the racket turning in your hand; too thin a handle is equally bad as it will also tend to slip through your grip. Where the weight is shown, select a racket weighing about 13 ounces for girls, 13½ ounces for boys and women, and 14 ounces for men. Beginners need not get an expensive nor a tightly-strung racket. Intermediates will like a better racket which is strung to medium tension. Advanced players generally prefer a tightly strung racket.

If there is no pro shop in your area, ask an experienced player to accompany you to a store and advise you. A medium weight racket for a man, a light weight racket for a woman, is the best choice for a beginner. Be sure that your racket is well strung. Nylon strings are less expensive and last longer. While gut strings are the advanced players' and champions' choice, they wear out more quickly. Sagging strings do not make for good tennis, and it costs no more to have a well-strung racket.

The weight of a racket may be distributed in three ways—evenly, top-heavy (heavier in the head than the handle) or handle-heavy. Tennis rackets are 27″ long, and the balance point is 13½″ up the handle. Most players like a racket balanced fairly evenly or slightly handle-heavy. Avoid a racket that is too heavy in the head; it is hard to manipulate when volleying and tends to swing through too fast on ground strokes.

Protect your strings from rain and wet balls. Keep your racket in a press when not in use. A small bottle of gut preserver will prolong the life of your strings.

TENNIS SHOES

There are any number of excellent tennis shoes on the market. Find yourself a pair with relatively thick ribbed or rough-surfaced soles. This will cushion your feet against the heavy wear and tear of fast running and jumping, and it will reduce fatigue. For the same reason it is best to wear heavy socks.

TENNIS BALLS

Good tennis requires good tennis balls. They are heavier and their flight is more easily controlled. In tournaments, new balls may be used as often as every seven or nine games, but the beginning player will find that a can of three balls will last quite a while. Replace them as soon as the nap wears off since worn balls cause a noticeably inaccurate flight.

All advanced players like to start a match with new balls, but they will use old balls for rallying or practicing on the backboard. Balls can be used anywhere from three sets to eight sets, although they are pretty well worn at the end of three sets on cement. Most advanced players will use balls three to five sets. Balls that are older can be used for backboard and service practice.

CLOTHING AND ETIQUETTE

A tennis player should appear on the court neatly attired, *always* in white.

The apparel for both men and women is all white. Tennis shoes with rubber soles are required on all tennis courts. Men wear a white shirt and white shorts, and women wear either shorts or tennis dress. The sweaters worn over tennis clothes can have color in them.

Common courtesy is not always as common around the court as you may expect or wish. Observe the careless or rude player who refuses to assist someone from an adjacent court in retrieving

Instead of flipping a coin for the choice of serve or side, the racket is spun on the tip of its head and allowed to drop. The decorative trim usually interwoven into the strings of the top and bottom of the head is "rough" on one racket face and "smooth" on the other.

ball that may have landed on his court. He may
ow his displeasure at seeing his game interrupted
 angrily hitting or kicking the ball instead of
turning it neatly to the waiting player on the next
urt.

Never argue with your partner, your opponent
 the umpire, or with linesmen, ballboys or spec-
tors. Be humble in victory and reasonable in de-
at.

In tennis, one shows consideration not only for
e's partner and one's opponents, but also for
ose who are playing on adjacent courts. Listed
elow are some of the rules of courtesy involved
 tennis.

1. Don't walk through someone's court while they
e playing a point. Wait until the point is over,
en run (not walk) across the court, preferably
ehind the baseline, to your court.

2. Don't talk or shout to a player while he is
 the middle of a point. Never talk to any player
ho is involved in a match until the match is over.

3. If a ball rolls into your court from an adjacent
urt, stop rallying (if you have not yet begun to

play) and return the ball immediately to one of
the people on the next court. If you are in the
middle of a point when the ball rolls through, you
either stop the point immediately if the ball dis-
turbs either you or your opponent, or you return
the ball as soon as the point is over.

4. Never ask a better player to play with you.
You may ask anyone who plays as well or worse
than you, but it is always the better player who
must ask the lesser one.

5. When your opponent is serving and the point
is over, if there are any balls on your side of the
court, pick them up quickly and return them directly to him. Do not return them wildly since you
may either hit him or force him to scramble to pick
up the balls.

6. If your opponent has served a fault, do not
go after the ball. Wait until his second serve is
over since an interruption between first and second
serves will disturb his rhythm.

7. Do not keep up a sustained conversation on
the court. It will not only bother your opponent
but also the people on the adjacent courts.

8. You are supposed to call all balls that bounce
on your side of the net. If you are in doubt as to
how to call a ball because you have not seen it
clearly, you can either ask your opponent to help
you on the call or you can play the point over.
Never call a ball on the opponent's side of the net
unless he asks you to help him.

9. It is better to err on calling "out" balls "in"
than on calling "in" balls "out." If a ball has
touched even a portion of the line, it is good.

10. When you have finished a practice set, always
thank your opponent, whether you have won or
lost. In doubles, thank your partner as well as your
opponents. In match play, shake hands with your
opponent; in match play doubles, shake hands with
your partner and then with both opponents.

There are many technical rules which involve
footfaults, interrupted play, resumption of interrupted matches, etc. Acquire a copy of the official

A handshake is traditional at the end of every match
n a tournament. It is not required when you are
imply practicing with a friend, but it is a friendly
gesture.

rules of the game so you can check on a particular ruling when in doubt. When playing tennis, *think* tennis, *play* tennis and don't talk about anything else.

COURTS

There are three major types of tennis court—*hard* courts, *clay* or *composition* courts, and *grass* courts. Lawn tennis was originally played on grass, as the name implies. In many countries it is impossible to use grass courts for various reasons. Though by far the most pleasant surface as far as foot fatigue is concerned, the ball skids and bounces low. Also, where clay or composition courts may improve with a little rain just before a match, grass courts stay wet too long.

All-weather courts are the most popular and most widely used. They include clay, ground brick dust and gravel-type courts as well as those with a topping, manufactured in different countries, intended to simulate these three. When they are maintained properly, all-weather courts have a good bounce, substantially higher and slower than grass courts.

Hard courts include wood (for indoor play), cement and asphalt. Many of the world's finest matches are played by professionals on canvas, which is taken by them from city to city and stretched over any level, hard surface in exhibition halls, ice hockey palaces, etc. Wood courts and slick cement ones are the fastest of all.

When playing on a gravel or clay-type court, be sure you repair any hole you inadvertently make with your shoes; smooth it with your toes.

TERMS IN TENNIS: STROKES

Tennis strokes are divided into three categories: *ground strokes, volleys* and *overhead strokes.* Ground strokes are those you play after the ball has bounced on your side of the net. The word "volley" is derived from the French *voler,* to fly. Thus, volleys are shots played when the ball is in flight, *before* it has bounced on your side of the net. Overhead strokes are those taken well above head-level.

Ground strokes comprise:

> *the drive*
>> (forehand and backhand)
> *the lob*
> *the dropshot*
> *the half-volley*

The half-volley is frequently used when you are on your way to net. It is played with the racket barely above the ground immediately after the ball bounces. Although it carries the name half-*volley,* it is in reality a *ground* stroke, as the ball has bounced before it is hit.

Volleys comprise:

> *the volley*
>> (forehand and backhand)

This is the Eastern forehand grip, often described a[s] [shak]ing hands with the racket:" the butt of the palm [is] on the **side** of the handle opposite the hitting fac[e of the] racket; the spread of the fingers aids in contro[l of] stroke.

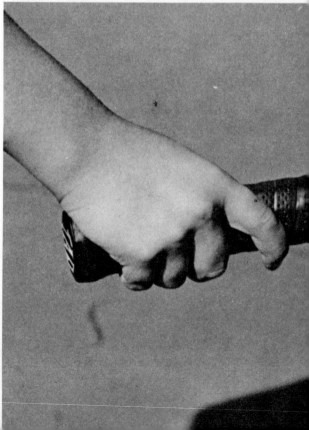

This is the Continental forehand, Continental b[ackhand,] Eastern backhand, the service and volley grip—all [one] and the same, with butt of palm resting on the **top** of the handle, one-quarter turn from the Eastern [grip.]

the drop volley
the drive volley
the lob-volley
Overhead strokes comprise:
the service
the smash

For the analytical reader, it is worth adding that
nnis strokes may be divided into *flat* strokes
strokes without spin), *topspin* strokes (shots which
e given a forward rotation) and *backspin* strokes
hich, as the name implies, move via an undercut
backward rotation. A topspin shot will tend to
ve the ball a fast, forward-spinning motion which
sults in a high bounce. The backspin strokes, ro-
ting the ball in backward direction, slow up the
ll; its bounce is lower. All three will be discussed
detail later.

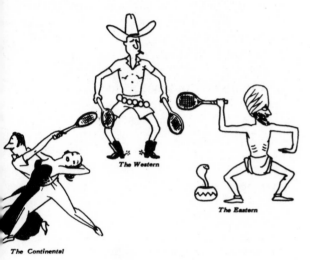

The Western

The Eastern

The Continental

THE GRIPS

Many names have been given to a great variety
f grips for the forehand. We recommend either
he *Eastern* grip or a *modified Continental*.

To understand how the Eastern grip functions,
ut your racket on the court on one edge, holding
he throat of the racket with the left hand to bal-
nce it. Now, with the right hand, shake hands with
he handle. Your fingers are slightly spread along
he handle and your thumb closes comfortably
round it.

The Continental grip, of which England's Fred
erry was the leading exponent, varies from the
astern grip in that the "V" formed by thumb and
rst finger is placed a little further to the left (about
ne-quarter of a turn). Although some players
laim that the Continental grip aids when hitting
rising ball, the majority of the world's finest
layers prefer the Eastern grip or a modified vari-
tion of it. The top Australian players of the last
ecade used the modified grip, which is approxi-
ately one-eighth turn left from the pure Eastern.

A grip we do not recommend is the Western.
Instead of putting your racket on the court on one
edge, place it flat. Now shake hands with the handle and you have the Western grip. Originating
in California, where the many cement and asphalt
courts cause a very high-bouncing ball, the Western
grip puts an undue strain on the elbow and wrist,
causes difficulties when playing backhand strokes
and when volleying, and is unsuitable for a low-
bouncing ball.

As the fastest way to better tennis, it is best to
ignore both the extreme Continental and the Western grips. As you make progress, you will develop
the grip that suits you best. Start with the Eastern
grip and let time do the rest. The less you have
to change your grip, the easier the game becomes.

Players who use the Continental style play forehand and backhand strokes without ever changing
their grip. Those who use an Eastern turn the
handle slightly for the backhand (no more than
one-quarter of a turn) to the right and place the
thumb, instead of around the handle, diagonally
along the handle. It gives support to the backhand
and it takes most of the strain of the impact off the
wrist. Try this grip. As soon as you are used to it,
you will agree that it gives maximum control over
your racket and over your stroke. Remember, it is
your left hand supporting the racket that enables
you to change your grip from forehand to backhand position.

In hitting a ground stroke, the wrist is laid back
slightly and is held with the least possible motion
throughout the hit. As the beginner advances, he
learns to use wrist motion, but the wrist is never
loose or wobbly. Controlled wrist motion is for the
advanced player, not for the novice.

The Eastern grip is suitable for all forehand
strokes and for learning volleys, overheads and service. Advanced players prefer the backhand grip
for the volley, service and smash, as it allows for
maximum wrist motion, which aids in the applica-
tion of power and spin to the ball. Grips and the
position or use of the hands may vary greatly. John
Bromwich of Australia used both hands on the handle for the backhand. Pancho Segura of Ecuador
uses both hands on the forehand. A few players,
such as Giorgio de Stefani and Beverly Fleitz, have
used no backhand. They shifted the racket from
right hand to left and played forehands on either
side. They paid the penalty when it came to rapid
exchanges at net.

CHAPTER 2

The Rules
Of The Game

The beginner should be familiar with the rules of tennis before he steps on the court.

The court is bounded by white lines, and any ball that touches the white line or lands within the area bounded by it is good. A ball is not called out until it bounces outside the court area; the beginner should therefore never catch a ball that is going out since it will automatically cost him the point.

The back line on either side of the court is called the *baseline;* the line running parallel to the baseline and the net is called the *service line;* the center line which runs perpendicular to the net and the service line is called the *center service line;* the outside lines that connect up the baselines are called the *alley lines;* and the long lines running parallel to the alley lines (four and one-half feet inside the alley lines) are called the *side lines.* Doubles is played in the entire court area. But the singles court is bounded by the side lines: any ball that lands between a side line and an alley line is out.

TENNIS SCORING

There are four or more points in a game and six or more games in a set. The points in a game are called *"15," "30," "40"* and *"game."* This is the equivalent of *"1," "2," "3"* and *"4."* A player must win a game by at least two points; if the score goes to 40-40, it is never called "40-40" but *"deuce."* One player now has to take two points in a row to win the game. The first point he gets is called *"ad"* or *"advantage."* If he does not win the next point, the score goes back to "deuce."

Whenever the score is announced, the server's score is given before the receiver's. Therefore if the server is leading by two points to one, the score is called "30-15." The word *"love"* signifies

zero or no points. If the server is leading by two points to none, for example, the score is called "30-love," or if the server is trailing by one point to three, the score is called "15-40."

The serve is alternated on every game. First one player serves an entire game and then his opponent serves an entire game. Whoever reaches six games first wins the *set,* although the set must be won by two games. A player can win a set by 6-0, 6-2, 6-3 or 6-4. He cannot win the set by 6-5, since the winner must always have two games more than the loser. A set may go to 7-5 or 8-6 or even 14-12. The players switch sides on odd games—after the first game, the third game, the fifth game, and so forth.

THE SERVE

The server stands on the base line in the right court and serves into the *service box* in the left court. If his ball does not fall into the service box, is called a *fault*. He is allowed a second serve. If the second ball does not fall into the service court, he has served a double fault and loses the point. He now moves to the left of the center service line and, standing on the baseline, serves into the service box diagonally opposite to him. If his serve does not go in, he is allowed a second serve. If he misses the second serve, he has lost another point. If the service ball touches the net but lands in the box, it is called a *"let"* and the serve is replayed. If the ball touches the net but does not land in the service box, he has served a fault.

The ball must be allowed to bounce in the service box before it is returned, the player losing the point if he does not return the ball over the net before the second bounce. The only time the ball must be allowed to bounce before the player returns it is on the service. Thereafter the receiver is allowed to hit the ball either after the first bounce or before the bounce. Any ball the player hits before it bounces is called a *volley* or an *overhead*.

MATCHES

Most matches are the best of three sets. Whoever wins two sets first wins the match. Sometimes each player will win a set and then the third set will be the decider. Only rarely are men required to play the best of five sets (whoever wins three sets first takes the match). Women are never required to play the best of five sets.

All women and all juniors (players 18 and under) are allowed to take a 10-minute rest after the second set. If one player wants to take the rest and the other does not, the rest is taken. If neither player wants a rest they can continue. In the best-of-five-set matches men may take a 10-minute rest at the end of the third set, unless both agree that they do not wish to take this intermission. The only exception to this rule is at Wimbledon (the All-England championships), where there is no intermission in a five-set match.

DOUBLES

In doubles, there are two players on each side. First one of the players serves a game, then one of the opponents serves a game. Then the first player's partner serves a game, and the second player's partner serves a game. The service must go into the service box diagonally opposite to the server. Thereafter, in doubles, any ball may be hit on or inside the farthest white lines that bound the court.

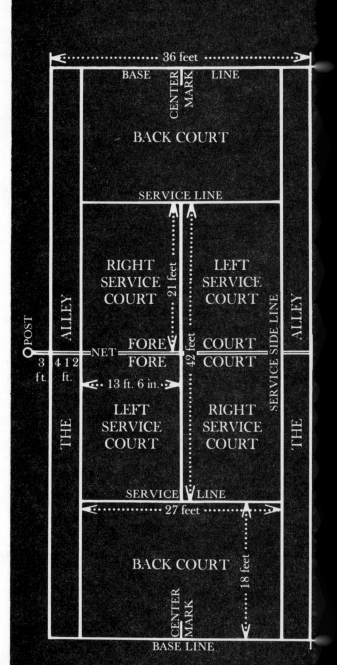

DIAGRAM AND DIMENSIONS
OF DOUBLES COURT

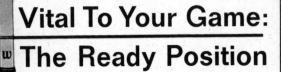

CHAPTER 3

Vital To Your Game: The Ready Position

Marty Riessen in the ready position for receiving servic[e]. His legs are spread, he shows concentration, his bo[dy] is bent and the racket is cradled in his left hand. Unli[ke] most players, Riessen's grip on the racket is not firm a[nd] the palm is not tight against the handle.

THE READY POSITION

The first comment you generally hear from a beginner who is watching a top tournament player is how little effort he seems to make to reach the ball. The better player anticipates the ball and starts earlier. He is ready for the next return; he is hardly ever caught by surprise. One can only achieve the ease and grace of the accomplished player by learning the *ready position*.

This position is not an inert, static pose; it is part of a motion. It is the equivalent of the starting position assumed by the sprinter waiting for the gun.

The mind is alert, the eyes are on the opponent and on the ball as soon as it is put into play, and the body is set to go into immediate action. Thus the ready position tremendously increases the chances of a good return. Analyze it, understand it and apply it—and you are on your way to becoming a good tennis player.

GRIP, RACKET AND STANCE

Let us assume that you have not played before. You take the forehand grip for the ready position. (A few players prefer to wait for the ball with a backhand grip. It is a matter of personal choice; the important thing is to get used to one or the other and to stick with it.)

In practice or in warm-ups prior to playing a set, your ready position is 12 to 18 inches behind the baseline in the center of the court, assuming that you are playing singles. The fingers of the left hand support the racket at the throat. The racket head is perpendicular to the ground and it stays that way during the stroke. Most players feel comfortable when the racket head points slightly to the backhand side, although an occasional player likes to point the racket directly in front of him (e.g., Tony Trabert). The racket does not go below the level of the right wrist during the stroke. For a low bouncing ball you simply bend the knees more deeply and make every effort not to let the wrist point down.

The body weight rests on the balls of the feet, which are placed comfortably 12 to 18 inches apart. This gives the player good balance and makes it possible to move quickly sideways or forward as necessary. The weight never rests on the heels at any time. The body is bent forward slightly through a flexing of the knees, and it is this which enables the player to get off to a fast start. He is prepared for instantaneous action in any direction. This is the ready position to be assumed before each stroke and after each stroke when there is sufficient time.

After you have learned the ready position, try moving in one direction by springing off from the opposite foot (from the left foot if going to your right). You do not run with the racket held stiffly in front of you; the shoulders pivot, bringing the racket to the right side for a forehand and to the left side for a backhand. The eye remains on the ball from the time it is in the opponent's hand or on his racket until the rally is over.

READY POSITION SEQUENCE

1. Racket is held in forehand grip always (or backhand grip always if that is your personal preference);

2. Left hand supports racket at its throat;

3. Racket head is perpendicular to the ground and points slightly toward backhand;

4. Knees are flexed;

5. Body bends forward slightly;

6. Weight is on balls of feet, which are parallel and well apart;

7. Eyes are on the ball at all times;

8. Push off with left foot when moving right, and vice versa;

9. Pivot shoulder and arms in direction toward which you will move.

Try the ready position, step by step, right now. Take a racket and follow the points one by one. Watch good players: even the hardest returns are often within their reach because they start in the proper ready position. Anyone who fails to acquire a proper starting position will never be a first class player. Start with it now and stay with it always. Without it you will fail in your timing, frequently be caught off balance and be late with your return.

The ready position is an *action*, not a passive stance. The movement of the ball, after it leaves your opponent's racket, determines in which direction your action continues. Comparing yourself with the sprinter, the ball leaving your adversary's racket is the starting gun.

If you want to be a good player, you must adopt a good player's habits from the very start. The ready position is the basis of better tennis. Only with utter concentration and long, hard practice can you reach the top. As in every sport, it is essential in tennis to understand the "how" and "why" of the game and then to apply your knowledge. The tendency of the beginner—and of too many players with years of tennis behind them—is to delay getting into action until the ball has passed the net, or even until after the ball has bounced. Watch average players who start their backswing too late and you will usually discover it is the lack of a ready position that caused the delay.

Decide now to make the proper ready position the first part of every stroke and to return to it immediately after every stroke. You will eliminate years of frustration and the biggest obstacle to better tennis.

How To Hit
The Forehand

In this series of pictures Eddie Moylan, a player's player with beautiful groundstrokes, is hitting a classical Eastern forehand with slight overspin. The first frame shows the start of the backswing just after Eddie has released his racket from his left hand in the ready position. The right foot has started to come back to place his body sideways to the net. The next two frames show successive phases of the backswing with the racket head drawn back slightly high and the right shoulder and arm pivoting backward so that the left shoulder faces the net. Knees and elbow are slightly bent. The fourth frame shows the end of the backswing and the start of the approach in a closed stance, with the weight mainly on the right foot. As Eddie swings forward (below left), his elbow straightens, the racket levels out and his weight shifts forward to the left foot. On the follow-through, the racket head again is raised; this action imparts the topspin so desirable for control. After the stroke (last frame) Eddie immediately resumes the ready position.

The forehand stroke, one flowing motion when properly executed, can be broken down into four component parts. A careful study of the four phases will assist the beginner in laying the foundation for an excellent stroke. It will also help the advanced player to improve his game. Through analysis of the four phases he can detect a flaw and learn how to overcome it.

PHASE I: THE BACKSWING

The player always starts with the ready position. The right shoulder and arms pivot while the head of the racket is brought slightly up and back. It remains perpendicular to the ground all the way and describes an arc until it points behind you. A few players draw the racket straight back (e.g., Dick Savitt), but the beginner will have a tendency to stop the stroke at the end of the backswing if he does not use the circular wind-up. This arc-like motion should be held to a minimum, since an overblown wind-up can result in a late hit. This phase of the stroke is known as the *backswing*. During the game, every stroke should be smoothly continuous, but now we will stop after each section of the stroke for the purpose of analysis.

PHASE II: THE APPROACH

The left foot is placed forward toward the approaching ball and toward the point of impact, and the left shoulder faces the net. The knees remain slightly bent and the weight rests mostly on the right foot. This part of the stroke is called the *approach* on the closed stance. (A discussion of the open stance, used by advanced players, will come later.)

PHASE III: THE HIT

Now the weight is shifted slowly from the right foot to the left foot, moving the right shoulder to-

ward the net. This shift of weight continues through the moment of impact. The ball is hit when it is a little closer to the net than the left foot. In other words, you are leaning forward to meet the ball. Your eyes are on the ball from the moment it leaves the opponent's racket until it lands on the center of the strings. This phase is called the *Hit*. You should feel like a baseball player swinging his bat, although a bat starts at shoulder level, whereas the racket moves at waist level.

PHASE IV: THE FOLLOW-THROUGH

The body weight is carried further until it rests on the left foot. The right foot serves for balance. The right shoulder follows netward with the weight of the body until arm and racket point toward the top of the opponent's backstop. In other words, the racket has moved from waist level to an upward or shoulder-level position across the net. The racket is still perpendicular to the ground. Your strings carry the ball forward and over the net. The longer the ball is felt on the strings, the better the stroke. This prolongs the moment of impact and assures greater accuracy, as well as a deep return. This most important phase of the forehand is called the *follow-through*.

WHERE TO HOLD THE RACKET

There are several schools of thought on where to grip the racket. Some players place the hand an inch above the bottom of the handle. This is a choke grip. Others prefer to hold the edge of the handle—the butt—in the palm of the hand. In the recommended grip, the butt end of the racket handle is even with the outside of the hand holding it. Take your racket in the forehand grip. If the racket butt rests in your palm, it reduces the control of your racket and you tend to whip the ball with your wrist. If, on the other hand, the handle protrudes an inch, you have a choke grip and you lose some of your reach. The third grip, with an even line from the side of the hand to the butt end of the racket, is the preferred one. A choke grip is sometimes used by a young player if the racket is too heavy. It is better for him to learn the recommended grip using a lightweight racket.

THE ELBOW

The arm is held in a natural position throughout the stroke. It is neither held out stiffly nor is it cramped by the body. It is slightly bent until, at the end of the follow-through, it straightens almost completely. In a rigid position (not desirable), the arm would stick out in a straight line; in a cramped position (also undesirable), the elbow would come close to touching the body. The arm should *reach* for the ball, but there should always be a certain amount of elbow bend.

Chuck McKinley moving to his right on the baseli[hits an Eastern forehand with plenty of topspin.

Tony Trabert gets down for a low forehand. He h[the ball well in front of him and strokes smooth[

...sley Turner "spoons" a forehand down the line ...laying back her wrist as she runs forward.

...ith practically a straight elbow just after the hit, ...is is a classic Eastern forehand.

THE WRIST

There is some slight wrist motion in a forehand, for otherwise you would simply "arm" the ball over the net. However, too much wrist motion causes loss of control. The arm should be relaxed and the wrist should be firm. If the wrist is at all loose at the moment of impact, the ball will move the racket instead of the racket moving the ball. The wrist is therefore firm at all times, but it moves slightly during the course of the stroke. Here is a good way to picture the wrist action in the forehand:

Position 1. Hold your arm straight in front of you so that wrist and arm form an absolutely straight line;

Position 2. Lay the wrist back slightly (wrist moves toward the right);

Position 3. Move the wrist forward again so that wrist and arm are once more in a straight line.

The wrist moves from Position 1 to Position 2 during the backswing. It stays in Position 2 (firmly) through the hit and through part of the follow-through. It reaches Position 3 at the end of the follow-through. This is extremely important for the beginner and the intermediate player. Only the very skilled can move from Position 2 to Position 3 *during* the hit. Any attempt to accomplish this earlier will result in an erratic, uncontrolled stroke. Trying to use wrist action before the player has had several years of experience is like suggesting a half-gainer to an elementary diver who has not yet learned a running jump.

THE STROKE

Now try hitting a forehand slowly with a short stop between each section of the stroke. Have someone read this aloud to you. Here we go:

1. The ready position—racket points slightly to the left but neither down nor up;

2. Racket travels upward and backward in a narrow arc as body pivots;

3. Wrist is laid back slightly (bent elbow does not hug body);

4. Left foot moves forward toward the ball and left shoulder is turned toward the net;

5. Body moves netward and weight shifts from right foot to left;

6. Racket meets ball squarely in front of body;

7. Weight follows through to left foot;

8. Racket sweeps upward toward top of opponent's fence;

9. Wrist and arm are in a straight line;

10. Racket head is still perpendicular to the ground;

11. Racket and feet move back to ready position.

Repeat the action again and again, each time reducing the stop between the four phases of the

Dennis Ralston stretches wide into the alley for what is probably a forehand return-of-serve. The footwork and balance are excellent. You get a clear view of his forehand grip, which is halfway between the Eastern and Continental, and is sometimes called the "Australian grip." The racket head is tilted slightly upward.

entire forehand stroke, phase by phase. Even the advanced player who has developed some flaw will do well to break down his stroke step by step. I will show what went wrong and how to correct it.

Make sure the racket head describes a narrow arc, and make sure it is not raised above the shoulder. The arc gives continuity of motion. If the racket is taken back in a straight line, there is a tendency to come to a dead stop at the end of the backswing. A continuous swing eliminates the pause. Whenever necessary, start your backswing while you are running. In the case of a hard hit ball, the backswing must start the moment the ball leaves the opponent's racket. Only when a ball is hit easy can you move to the ball and then start the backswing. Do the footwork and the proper lining up for the shot before the forward phase of your groundstroke begins.

stroke until gradually all are blended into one motion. It is important never to lose balance by standing too straight, or by bending from the waist, or by moving forward with shoulder and arm while hips do not follow through. As soon as you feel that something has gone wrong, stop and repeat the

Young Tony Trabert starts a forward swing on a closed stance, Eastern grip, overspin forehand, just inside the baseline. The legs are well spread and the weight is even on both feet (the camera has caught Tony just as his weight is shifting from right to left). The racket head is at a perfect height and is not too high. Tony uses plenty of topspin for control on both forehand and backhand drives.

CHAPTER 5

How To Practice Hitting A Tennis Ball

This demonstration, which is letter-perfect, embodies many of the same techniques used in practicing the forehand.

If you are a beginner eager to start out the right way, save yourself time and frustration by asking a good player to assist you. Imagine a circle approximately three feet in diameter just to the right of center of the court and near the baseline. It is in this area that you are going to hit the ball. Your assistant should stand on the same side of the net as you with a basket of tennis balls, which he is going to throw to you underhanded for better control. When you first start you should not have to worry about the oncoming ball as you will need all your concentration for the stroke itself. Once you can coordinate your backswing, footwork, for-

SALEM LUTHERAN CHURCH & SCHOOL
SOUTHEAST AT BEECHER AVE.
JACKSONVILLE, ILLINOIS 62650

Eddie Moylan demonstrates the beautiful classical Eastern backhand. He is in perfect ready position facing the net, with his legs apart and his knees slightly flexed. He waits with a forehand grip, racket cradled in the left hand.

Moylan starts his backswing and moves to the ball. He steps off on his right foot, not the left, because he has judged the ball will arrive two steps away. The pivot has started—right shoulder moves forward, left shoulder back.

ward motion and follow-through with the oncoming ball, you have made tremendous progress. Only then should you have someone play the ball to you from the other side of the net.

GETTING SET

Start with the *ready position* facing the net with your feet 12 to 18 inches apart, knees bent, back straight and weight on the balls of your feet; hold the racket with a forehand grip, the throat of the racket gently cradled in the fingers of the left hand; the racket face is perpendicular to the ground, the racket head tilted very slightly upward and pointing to your left (in the direction of your opponent's forehand alley). Flex your knees several times so that you get the impression of being bouncy although your feet do not actually leave the ground. You are in perfect balance. This preparation before the stroke is an absolute necessity. Imagine a boxer standing flat-footed with feet together and arms at his side; he would be a sitting duck.

THE PIVOT

The *body pivot* to your right begins as soon as the ball leaves the hand of your helper. The right shoulder turns sideways so that the left shoulder points to the net. This shoulder pivot pulls the arms, racket, and knees rightward. Any delay in the pivot will make you late with the hit. As the pivot finishes, the *backswing* begins. It is all one smooth, continuous motion. The fingers of the left hand drop away from the racket and the right arm moves slowly backward. The arm is slightly bent during the backswing, but the elbow never touches the body from the time the backswing begins. At the end of the backswing, the racket face is perpendicular to the ground at waist-level and is pointing toward the fence directly behind you. The wrist is broken backward slightly so that racket and arm *do not* form a straight line. The arm is relaxed and slightly bent, but the wrist is firm and will not move at any point during the hit.

25

The step on the left foot is completed and the right shoulder is fully forward. The racket head has reached head height and is still cradled in the left hand at the throat. Note the spread of the fingers on the grip.

The right foot is now crossing over and the back swing is at its highest point. The racket is still held in the left hand. The knees bend until the ball is hit. The weight is starting to shift forward to the right foot as it crosses over.

NETWARD MOTION

The *netward motion* now begins. There should be no pause between end of backswing and start of netward motion. It is all one continuous action. At first you may have difficulty timing the ball and will have to rush or delay your netward motion. However, after eight or ten balls have been thrown to you, you will get the rhythm. In the netward motion, the arm and racket come netward as the weight is transferred to the left foot. As the racket and arm move toward the ball, the left foot steps toward the net. The body is almost sideways to the net, but the left foot is still *to the left* of the right foot. Simultaneously the left foot moves netward, the weight moves netward and the right arm and racket move netward. Do not let your left foot cross beyond your right foot, or your weight and balance will be moving sideways rather than netward.

26

THE HIT

As your left foot steps netward, your *racket meets the ball* slightly in front of and to the right of your body. The arm is slightly bent, the racket face is perpendicular to the ground and is at waist-level; the wrist is kept broken slightly and is absolutely firm at the moment of impact.

If the wrist should wobble as you hit, the ball will move your racket instead of your racket moving the ball. If your racket head is tilted down, you will shove the ball instead of stroking it. If your wrist is not broken, you have no margin of safety: you would have to hit the ball exactly at your side, for if you caught it early the ball would go shooting off to your opponent's forehand alley, and if you caught it late it would go shooting off to your opponent's backhand alley. When the wrist is laid back, your margin of safety is great—you can still hit the ball well if you catch it late or early.

This is the start of the foward swing, with right foot planted forward, right shoulder forward, racket head slightly laid back and down from its high point but still above wrist, knees well bent and elbows starting to straighten.

This is the start of the follow-through. The arm is straight, the weight completely on the front foot, as the body and legs are straightening up. Note that the left arm has straightened out in back, which is a natural action as the weight moves forward.

FOLLOW-THROUGH

You have now made contact with the ball slightly in front of and to the right of your body, and your *follow-through* begins. There is no pause, of course, between hit and follow-through; follow-through is simply a continuation of the total motion. Your arm and racket continue their natural sweep, moving forward and upward. At the conclusion of the follow-through, the arm and racket are almost one straight line (the wrist is no longer broken), the racket points toward the top of your opponent's fence and your weight is completely on the left foot. The knees are slightly flexed but the back is straight (you would be falling forward off balance if your back were bent). The high follow-through has made you lift up on the ball, and this has given your shot topspin. Without topspin, your ball would sail straight into the net (topspin lifts it over), or if it cleared the net it would not drop

until gravity pulled it down.

As soon as the follow-through has been completed you hop back into the ready position. You are now ready to pivot for the next shot.

THEN ALL TOGETHER

If you are having any problem with pivot, forward motion, hit or follow-through, try the whole procedure without a ball. Let your assistant pretend to throw you a ball, then go through the motions of the stroke. Remember:

• have that bounce in the ready position;

• keep your balance at all times;

• hold your wrist firm but leave your arm relaxed;

• keep your racket head from dropping or cocking upwards;

• follow-through high while retaining balance;

• hop back immediately for the next shot.

This is the end of the follow-through. The racket head is again at head height, pointing to the opposite fence. It shows the end of the full swing. Moylan should now immediately return to the ready position.

If you are having a problem with taking too big a backswing, correct it by hardly taking the racket back at all. If your tendency is to drop your racket head, cock it upward a few times. If your follow-through is too big and ends around your left shoulder, stop your follow-through immediately after the hit. Corrections are made by exaggerating in the opposite direction.

With your assistant standing on your side of the net, the element of surprise has been taken out of the game and you can devote all your efforts to perfect stroking, perfect timing and perfect balance. When you feel sufficiently confident, your assistant should go to the other side of the net. You will find the problems increasing as soon as the ball comes to you at varying speed, varying height and in a different place each time.

Until you completely master those balls thrown at you in the imaginary circle, there is no point in starting to chase balls all over the court. It will ruin your stroke, your timing, your balance and your confidence. Build up your stroke and build up your confidence. During the first few practice sessions, if your teacher-assistant throws the ball outside your reach, make the complete motion of the forehand stroke even without hitting the ball. Finish the stroke as though you were hitting the ball. Remember, it is the stroke that matters. Never mind the ball. Execute a perfect stroke each time and the results will be perfect. Too many beginners have but one object—to hit the ball, somehow, somewhere, without thought of the development of style. As a result, bad habits can be formed that are difficult to correct.

is not only better for your game but *much more
n* to try to do it correctly.

SUMMARY

Study tennis. Understand the reason for all the
hases of the stroke. Stop when you begin making
rrors and analyze where in the course of the
troke you have failed. Be able to repeat the steps
o yourself. Practice them without a ball in front
f a mirror to see if you can catch a fault. Above
ll, don't try to advance too fast or you will lose
he fun of acquiring a perfect stroke.

The primary purpose of this chapter has been
o teach you to execute a proper stroke each time,
ith proper backswing, footwork, timing, follow-
hrough and balance. These elements, however
omplicated they may seem to the beginner, will
oon blend into an easy movement which you can
epeat automatically, without having to think about
ach part. To be able to execute the forehand
roperly you must practice, practice, practice. Even
ithout a court you can practice your swing. The
w weeks you may devote to this procedure will
y a lifetime of dividends. It will mean the dif-
rence between playing awkwardly and getting
scouraged or playing gracefully and enjoying the
arning process. In the one case you may never pass
yond the rank of beginner, but in the other case
ur improvement is unlimited. With constant prac-
ce you will reach the point where the stroke be-
mes automatic and you can then move on to the
xt chapter.

Chuck McKinley demonstrates the follow-through of a
backhand volley close to the net. On a volley hit above
net level with some underspin, the punch is downward and the racket ends lower than the ball. The
legs are well apart and the left arm is out for balance.
McKinley hit this ball with the racket head higher
than the wrist, but wrist action to control the ball
brought the head below wrist level.

How To Practice
Elementary Rallying

You have learned to hit a forehand while stan
ing in place. You are confident of your stroke an
you have the rhythm of *pivot, step-and-hit, follo*
through and *return-to-position*. You are boun
and you are watching the ball. You are now read
to rally certain easily hit balls. Do not try to a
vance too quickly, as it may cause you to forget t
basic principles of the stroke in your anxiety to h
the ball.

You are now going to move *to* the ball—sideway
forward, or a combination of both. At first yo
may overrun the ball, which means that you wi
have to cramp your elbow in order to hit it. A
other times you may misjudge the ball by planti
your feet too far from it, and you will then lo
your balance as your body stretches for it. Ther
fore you want to hit balls that require the lea
amount of running. This will teach you the feelir
of moving toward the ball without discouragir
you.

Take your position slightly behind the cent
service line. Your assistant or coach stands slight
behind the opposite center service line. His ba
must go short into your service court, which mea
he cannot hit it hard. In the beginning, you a
only required to clear the net. Do not worry abo
hitting to him or away from him. Simply conce
trate on getting to the ball and making a comple
stroke.

SKIP TO THE BALL

The ball is going to be hit a few steps away fro
you—to your right and perhaps well in front of yo
You are neither going to walk to the ball nor a
you going to run to it. You are going to *skip* to i
The skip motion allows you to hop to the ball an
step forward as you hit. It prevents you from bei
flat-footed and it keeps you bouncy. It is a motio
used by just about every good player when he do
not have to run too far to reach the ball. Again yo
start from the ready position, facing the net wit
feet apart and knees flexed. You bounce on you
left foot. Do not hop so high that your foot leav

e ground. You have been bouncy on the balls of
oth feet; now you let your weight descend on the
hole of the foot (your knees bend more deeply)
nd you push off with it toward your right.

So far you have pushed off with your left foot
nd stepped onto your right. Now the left foot is
rought close to the right foot and again the left
nee bends and pushes the body off to the right. If
ou are doing this correctly, you will find that you are
ipping sideways, with the left knee bending deeply
nd the left foot being used as the pusher. You will
robably not require more than two of these side-
ays skips to reach the ball. With the last push of
ur left foot, your right foot is planted where you
ink you should be to meet the ball—and you find
at now you are in the exact ready position. All
ou have to do is pivot, take your backswing, step
rward with your left foot as you hit, and follow
rough.

The beauty of the sideways-skip motion is that it
ways lands you in the perfect ready position. You
ay misjudge the ball the first few times by moving
o close or not close enough, but this is rather
sily corrected. If you are overrunning the ball, try
 take it too far away from you. If you are stretch-
g too far for it, try to overrun it.

Review the skip method of reaching the ball:
is a push-off with the left foot, a planting of the
ght foot, another deep-knee push-off with the left
ot and another planting of the right foot until
u reach the ball. Then you pivot, stroke and step
 with the left foot. If you are doing this correctly,
u will find yourself moving to the ball easily and
oking well.

PRACTICING THE SKIP

Practice the skip method in front of a mirror
til it becomes a natural motion. If you are con-
sed, think of it as skipping sideways; watch the
od players skip into position; ask your assistant
 coach to tell you if you are executing it correctly.
You can now move to a position one step behind
e center of the baseline. Your opponent can either
nd on his service line or stand at net to volley
ur returns. Again your only object is not to hit
 or away from your opponent but simply to clear
 net. Your assistant will try not to hit the ball
rd, but you will have to get ready sooner and
ve faster. The same routine of ready position,
eways skip and stroke is repeated. You must push
 with your left foot as soon as the ball leaves
ur opponent's racket. You are now able to handle
st balls that are not hit too far away from you.
en you are hitting them over the net regularly
hout losing balance and without neglecting any
ase of your stroke, your assistant can begin to
ve back. Pretty soon both of you are standing

There is no pause between the end of the backswing . . .

on your baselines and you are having good rallies.

Your object in these rallies is to clear the net by
a considerable margin. Do not try to hit hard. Your
opponent is hitting easily to you and you should be
able to return most of the balls. If you have problems, move back up to the service line until you
work them out.

You are going to improve rapidly in these rallying sessions. Within a very short time, you will be
able to hit 10, 15 or 20 balls back over the net without missing. You should be clearing the net by at
least eight feet. In two or three days you should be
rallying reasonably well against soft balls. Whenever you have a lapse, move to the service line
and review the fundamentals.

. . . and the start of the forward motion

31

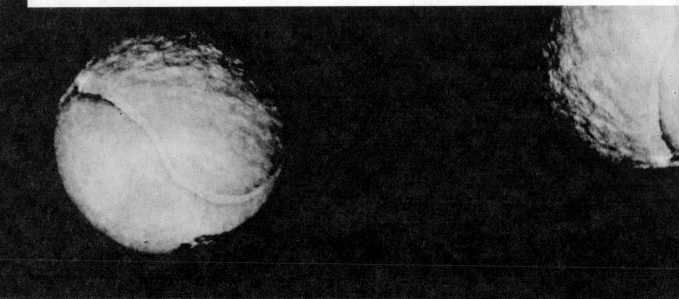

Pitfalls

During the course of learning there is the constant danger of lapsing into stroke or rallying error. If you are aware of these danger spots, you have won half the battle:

1. *Your weight is moving backward;* it should move into the ball.

2. *Your racket head is dropping;* it should be perpendicular to the ground.

3. *The racket facing is opening;* the ball will swoop upwards.

4. *Your wrist is floppy;* the ball is moving your racket instead of your racket moving the ball.

5. *Your arm and wrist are a straight line;* the wrist should be broken slightly.

6. *Your follow-through is at waist-level;* it should end with the racket head pointing toward the top of your opponent's back fence.

7. *Your follow-through is too big;* you are off balance at the finish of the stroke.

8. *You are failing to get back immediately into the ready position;* you will not be ready for the next shot.

9. *You are standing too straight;* your knees should be flexed.

10. *You are bending from the waist;* you are top-heavy and off balance.

11. *Your elbow is too close to your body on the hit;* you are cramping the ball.

12. *Your arm is absolutely straight on the hit;* this is an unnatural position except when stretching to retrieve a wide ball.

13. *You are catching the ball behind you;* your wind-up is too late.

14. *You are hitting the ball as it drops;* take it at the top of the bounce.

15. *You are finishing with your left foot pointing sideways;* your left foot should never cross over.

16. *You are finishing with your right foot forward;* the left foot should always be closer to the net than the right.

17. *Your backswing is too big;* it throws you off balance.

18. *Your follow-through is too short;* a high follow-through will give the ball topsin.

19. *You are standing flat-footed;* you should always be on the balls of your toes.

20. *You are taking short little running steps toward the ball;* skip sideways toward a ball that is not too far away from you.

21. *You are reaching the ball with your left foot forward;* the sideways skip will prevent this from happening.

22. *You are hitting the ball too hard;* the object should be to clear the net by a wide margin.

23. *You are missing the ball too often;* you are taking your eye off of it.

Most of these rules apply to all players, but a few are specifically for the beginner. The advanced player may hit on the rise, with spins, with an open stance, with wrist action and with more pace. The beginner who tries any of these tactics will never learn the basic drive and never have consistency. You don't play cadenzas before learning the scales.

How To Use A Backboard

In Practice

You have had several lessons. You have learned to stroke a forehand from a stationary position. When your forehand has been grooved so that you do not forget the ready position, pivot, backswing, forward motion, hit and follow-through, you have tried rallying from just behind the service line. You have learned to skip sideways toward the ball and to hit it with a large margin of safety over the net. You are able to rally from the back court against relatively soft shots, and you can generally hit 15 or 20 balls over the net consecutively. You are now sufficiently advanced to play a game against the backboard and to get something out of it.

Most tennis clubs and public courts have a practice wall or backboard. Next to the helping hand of a coach or assistant, a wall is ideal for your practice. Use it as often as you can.

You will find that you must not hit the ball too hard against the wall at first; the harder you hit, the faster the ball comes back to you. You will also notice that you cannot take your backswing as slowly as you did against a tossed ball or against a gently hit shot. There is simply not enough time. The backboard will therefore teach you to get into position much more quickly. Once you are used to wall practice, you will find it an excellent means of perfecting a shot.

HOW THE BACKBOARD WORKS

Practice against a wall has several purposes: it grooves a shot, it teaches you to get ready quickly, it gives you better timing and it makes you steadier. It is also fun. The ball always comes back, and after 15 or 20 minutes you have had a real workout. It will help you improve far more than rallying against an unsteady player—the backboard never misses.

There is a method to practice. There is no point in going out to the wall and being sloppy. Follow the method and you will see the immediate improvement in your technique and in your steadiness.

Always start the ball from the ready position. Face the wall with feet apart and knees flexed. Pivot your shoulders, start your backswing and at the same time drop the ball in front of you to your right. If there is a line drawn on the wall at net level, hit the ball a good 8 or 10 feet above it. If there is no line, imagine one. Do not hit the ball hard; it will come rocketing back at you before you are ready and you will find yourself pushing instead of stroking it.

The wall is fast. There is no time to hold your follow-through. As soon as your swing is finished, be ready to hit the next ball. When the ball accidently comes to your backhand, don't try to hit it. Instead, hop backwards three or four steps and hit it on your forehand. To do this you stand sideways, push off with your right foot and land on your left. When

moving to your right, push off with your left foot and land on your right. In both cases, you will be able to pivot and step in with your left foot.

Since this is a relatively speedy game, you will find that results will be best if, after starting the ball from the ready position, you maintain thereafter a sideways position to the wall. You can then hop to your right or to your left as necessary.

WHERE TO STAND

You do not need new balls for wall practice. Take six or eight old ones, since you may lose quite a few that go sailing over the wall. Stand far enough away from the wall so that you are not being rushed (about the distance from baseline to net). At first the ball may bounce short; simply take it on the second or third bounce. As you become more adept at wall practice, the ball will come to you so that you can hit it on the first bounce. Hit it on the second bounce if you have to, but never hit it on the first bounce when the ball has started to drop. Instead, move toward the ball and hit it at the top of the bounce. Always try to hit the ball when it is a good six inches in front of you so you can move toward it.

Good players can hit the ball on the half-volley or on the rise. Beginners should not try these strokes. Never attempt to hit the ball just after it has bounced and before it has risen. It is much better for you to hop back two steps, then step in to meet the ball with your left foot. The first time you jump into a swimming pool you don't try a swan dive, and the first few months on a practice wall don't attempt the advanced strokes.

Your first objective on the wall is to groove your stroke. If the ball comes to you too quickly, stop it but don't try to stroke it. Review the various steps of the stroke in your own mind, then check yourself to see if you have fallen into any error. The backboard also helps you hop to the ball. It teaches you consistency. Give yourself a goal each day—hitting five balls in a row, then 10, then 20, then 30.

ADVANCED RALLYING

After several backboard sessions in which y⦵ have learned to hit the ball back with reasonab⦵ consistency, you can get further forehand practi⦵ by having someone play the ball to you. You w⦵ now have to cover a lot more ground.

Avoid getting on the court with another to⦵ beginner; you will spend more time picking ⦵ balls than hitting them. Find a teacher or frie⦵ to coach you for a while who will hit balls ⦵ rather than away, from you. Your object shou⦵ be to get the ball over the net by a clearance ⦵ eight or ten feet while still not neglecting footwo⦵ stroking, balance and skipping. As long as yo⦵ opponent does not hit the ball too hard, you shou⦵ be able to return it with reasonable consistency.

In addition to all the elements that go into t⦵ making of a perfect swing in perfect time, with bo⦵ weight, balance and follow-through all properly ⦵ counted for, there remains the somewhat disturbi⦵ factor that the tennis player must hit an object ⦵ motion. Not only an object in motion but with ⦵ opponent whose aim it is to play the ball outsi⦵ your reach. Consider this and you will understa⦵ how important it is to groove your stroke so th⦵ you do not have to think about how to hit the ba⦵

By practicing enough you will develop a sou⦵ stroke which you should try to use even under t⦵ most difficult of circumstances. Only when the stro⦵ is automatic can you develop variations—spi⦵ loops and chips. The basic drive must be acquir⦵ first.

ANTICIPATING

Anticipation is developed through proper pre⦵ aration. By assuming the ready position after eve⦵ stroke, you are prepared to go anywhere, to be an⦵ where for the return. The knees must be flexed a⦵ the feet ready to push off in any direction. Y⦵ move as soon as the ball leaves your opponen⦵ racket, your backswing starts as you run, and t⦵ racket begins to come forward just before the ba⦵ bounces (earlier on a fast ball).

Every player is likely to develop a stroke a⦵ game which suits his physical and mental make-u⦵ although many a steady young player becomes ⦵ aggressive one as he grows older. It is better as⦵ beginner to be steady. Unfortunately too ma⦵ players have a tendency to hit hard and to forg⦵ the stroke, balance and timing. Their game is a wi⦵ one, with an occasional sizzler. This is extreme⦵ poor tennis. Style and accuracy come first. Antici⦵ tion, footwork, balance and timing should abso⦵ your concentration for a long time. Only after y⦵ know how to stroke the ball and where to place ⦵ should power enter into your game. The hard-hi⦵ ting tactics of the beginner are his worst obsta⦵

A tennis machine is a friend indeed

good tennis. He will acquire bad habits which are nearly impossible to change later.

The steady player keeps in mind the importance of hitting the ball on the top of the bounce and in front of the body. This will lead eventually to more aggressive play as his game matures.

THE TENNIS MACHINE

After the initial practice sessions with coaches, friends and on the backboard, you may want to use the excellent tennis machines which are achieving increasing popularity. These throw from 50 to 00 balls on the spot of your choice on the court, one at a time. Again, one must have a method in order to get the most out of this type of practice.

First, the balls can be aimed so that they bounce ightly in front of your body. You need only pivot, roke, follow-through and return to the ready position. It is a very good way of grooving the stroke. Secondly, stand three feet to the side of where the all is going to bounce. As it leaves the machine, you kip to the ball, pivot, hit and return to your orig-

inal position. This is repeated until you have learned to move easily and gracefully to the ball while still stroking well. Third, the machine is directed to hit a series of short balls. Here you can practice running up, planting your right foot and stroking. Get back to your original position, making no attempt to hit the next ball, then run up again for the third ball.

Hitting forehands is more than just stroking; it is running as well. The machine can be set to provide you with both stroke and running practice. And like the backboard, the machine does not miss.

You now have a coach, friends, backboard and possibly a machine against which to work. As your game progresses and your consistency improves, you try for depth while still maintaining a good margin of safety over the net. Your aim should now be to hit the ball within two or three feet of the baseline. You have emerged from the rank of novice and you are about to learn control through depth and placement.

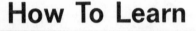

CHAPTER

8

How To Learn

The Backhand

One of the simplest methods of learning a clas backhand is to practice the stroke with a tw handed grip. This automatically eliminates common stroke defects of the "bad" backhand. A when the beginner is ready to hit one-handed, simply drops his left hand away and the stroke there. He will find the backhand even easier learn than the forehand because he now knows ready position, the weight shift and how to ma contact with the ball.

THE GRIP

The backhand grip is achieved by shaking han with the racket (the Eastern forehand), then tu ing the handle one-quarter to the right. The thu is placed diagonally along the handle and t fingers are spread slightly. This grip is not us exclusively for the backhand; as the beginner a vances, he will also use this grip for serve, ov head and volley. The grip is firm but the arm relaxed (most beginners tend to have a relaxed g and a tight arm). The butt of the racket handle level with the outside of the hand. To make t grip a two-handed one, place the left hand i mediately above the right so that the two han touch in the manner of a left-handed baseb batter.

The racket should be held tightly with the finge If the grip is at all loose, the ball will make t racket twist in the hand.

THE READY POSITION

The player is in the ready position. He has forehand grip and the throat of the racket is gen cradled in the fingers of the left hand. He is faci the net, his feet are apart and his knees are flex As he sees the ball coming to his backhand, his l hand holds the racket while his right hand mov to the backhand grip. Then, as his shoulders mo to the left, to get ready for the hit, the left ha moves down the racket until it touches the rig hand. The racket is at waist level and is movi backwards while the shoulders pivot. When t backswing is completed, the racket will still be waist-level and the racket head will point towa the player's back fence.

THE RACKET HEAD

The player is going to hit the ball with his si toward the net. The racket head, which was waist-level pointing to the player's back fence, w move forward and *upward*, so that at conclusi of the stroke the racket head will be pointing ward the top of the opponent's fence. At no poi in the stroke is the racket head ever dropped that it points to the ground. At no point is t racket head ever cocked upward. It remains p pendicular to the ground at all times. This mea

Rosewall's legs are facing the fence, but he has twisted his hips and waist around to make an underspin
recovery on a wide shot. A very firm wrist is required to control this ball, but Rosewall can hit it anywhere in the
court from this position. He is considered to have one of the best backhands in the game.

face of the racket (the strings) is never tilted
forward.

FEET, ARMS AND BODY

At the conclusion of the backswing, the shoulders
have pivoted so that the top of the body faces the
alley line and the racket is pointing to the rear
fence. Both feet are pointing to the alley but no
step has been taken yet. The feet have simply
pivoted from their net-facing position to a leftward
position. As the player is about to hit, his right foot
will step forward (toward the net) so that the
body will then be completely sideways to the net.
As he makes this step with his right foot toward
the net, his weight transfers with him from left foot
to right and he meets the ball not only with his
racket but with his weight as well.

The arms are slightly bent throughout the back-

swing and hit. They straighten only at the finish,
when the racket is pointing to the top of the opponent's fence. This is true for both the two-handed
and the one-handed backhand.

The only difference between the two-handed
and the one-handed shot is the moment of impact. When the ball is hit with two hands, it is
taken very slightly in front of the body. Later, when
the player learns to hit with one hand, the ball will
be taken one to two feet in front of the body.

THE WRIST

In the backhand stroke, the arm, wrist and racket
form a straight line. The wrist is not laid back nor
does it lead. It is firm throughout the stroke. This
means that the backhand is hit with the shoulder,
arm and racket, rather than with any wrist action.

37

Lew Hoad is just taking a last step into position as he is caught in the middle of his backswing, eyes glued on the ball.

Hoad's front (right) foot is in position, but weight is still on his back foot. Racket draws back at head height. Knees bent.

The backhand is one smooth stroke—ready position, grip change and pivot, backswing, step, hit and follow-through. There is no hesitation or pause between any of the steps. All is one unified movement.

THE DANGER SPOTS

The player should check his stroke carefully to see if he is guilty of any of the following errors:

1. *Arm too far from the body*. The right arm should never be stiff, not in the ready position, the backswing or the hit. The elbow comes closest to straightening immediately after the hit and at the follow-through. The elbow is not tucked into the body, but neither is it held away; it is in normal position, just as one would hold it when shaking hands.

2. *Body bending from the waist*. The bend should always be from the knees. The back is straight at all times and the legs are flexed. Low balls are hit from a deep knee-bend position, but the lower you bend, the farther the legs should be spread. If you concentrate on keeping the feet apart, it is easier to

The hit is perfect; it is in front of the body. Racket head is above wrist level. arm has straightened, weight is forward.

Hoad has guided the ball down the line (toward the camera) by holding back on the crossover follow-through.

Hoad is beginning his forward swing. Note how far around his right shoulder is. The open racket face indicates a wristy action.

Here is a better view of the open racket. You can see now that Hoad must flip his wrist over before he contacts the ball.

t a natural knee-flexing action. Bending from the aist causes the player to be off balance; it is hard r him to hit the ball with pace and it is awkward r him to regain the ready position.

3. *Too high a backswing.* The higher the back-ing, the greater the tendency to undercut the ll. The basic backhand is a drive. A slice (which hit with an open face) is a secondary shot, to be arned only after the drive is acquired. Later, as e player's backhand becomes grooved, he may oose to take a semi-circular wind-up. This figure-8

action often helps a player's rhythm, but the hit always starts from a low (waist-level) position and ends upward at the follow-through.

4. *Elbow leading on the hit.* This is the defect most common to those who have had no instruction. It is the rare player who can learn pace and ac-curacy from this kind of a backhand. There are two ways to overcome this tendency. One is to hit two-handed, starting at waist-level and ending high, with both arms straight. The other is to think in terms of throwing the right arm from one's own rear fence

This is an excellent follow-through. The racket is pointed at the ball, the weight is well forward and the pivot is completed.

This stance shows the full, free swing at the conclusion of the shot. Hoad will be jumping back into the ready position.

Chuck McKinley, like Ken Rosewall on page 38, is retrieving a backhand while facing the fence. The mastery this action is a sign of complete wrist control; Chuck knows he can hit from anywhere on his backhand. This not a shot for beginners.

to the top of the opponent's fence, with the shoulder as the pivot. The key word is *shoulder*.

5. *Shot ending at waist-level.* The stroke begins at waist-level but the racket and arm must end high in order to give the ball topspin. If the follow-through is low, the ball is flat—there is no overspin to lift it over the net or to bring it down into the opponent's court. The flat shot is likely to hit the net or, if it clears the net by too much of a margin, to sail out of court. There is no margin of safety in such a shot. Topspin gives the player control and a safety margin.

6. *Player holding follow-through too long.* As soon as the shot is over, the player must hop back into the ready position. A single shot seldom ends a point, and even what looks like a sure winner may sometimes come back. Being prepared is the key to good tennis.

THE BACKHAND SLICE

The topspin backhand should start low and e high; the slice backhand should start high and e low. In the topspin shot, the face of the racket perpendicular to the ground at the moment of i pact; in the underspin or slice shot, the racket fa is open at the hit.

There are times when the backhand drive is n the proper shot. It is always correct in elementa and intermediate tennis, but in the more advance game the player has to learn how to handle a lo bouncing short ball by slicing and coming in net behind the shot.

The slice is a more defensive weapon than t topspin backhand. The underspin causes the ba to hang in the air, which means it is an easi ball for the net man to volley. The topspin shot therefore more desirable, since it can be hit hard and it does not rise up to the net man.

arry MacKay (above) is "drawing the bow" on his
ckhand wind-up—an excellent picture of the start
the backhand on the baseline. There is a good
oulder turn, knees are bent, legs are spread and
e racket is still cradled, although its face is some-
hat too open.

Tony Trabert (below) has just finished the hit on a
great backhand. Tony puts overspin on this shot by
coming up on the ball as he hits, and he has plenty
of power and excellent control, partly due to putting
his thumb along the handle.

CHAPTER 9

How To Serve

Mike Sangster's serve is a classic of easy grace and power. At the end of the toss, his left arm is straight and pointing at the ball. The racket head is high and his elbow is bending (the racket head will drop down his back), his left foot is toeing the baseline and his right foot, which started further back, is now brought up close to the left as he prepares to bring his full power into the ball. His body is arched.

The service is the one stroke in which the player has complete control. He, not his opponent, manipulates the ball. If the server errs in accuracy, control or pace, he has only himself to blame. He can develop a forceful, reliable delivery through careful study of the stroke and through many hours of practice. It is the one stroke which he can practice without need of an opponent at any time. It is also the most important single stroke in tennis since, if it is aggressive and accurate enough, it can win point after point for the player on his service games.

Every part of the service is important—the stance, the grip, the toss, the wrist action and the transfer of body weight. The beginner should learn a simplified version of many of these elements, since he cannot acquire all the nuances of a big delivery during his first efforts. Once he has a grooved, consistent "beginner" serve, he can slowly add those elements which will give him more spin control and power.

The fun of tennis is to be able to get the ball in court just as soon as possible and before one gets discouraged. The beginner will enjoy learning the serve much more if he starts on the service line rather than the baseline; the ball will go in immediately. After three or four good serves, he can move back a few feet. By the end of 10 or 15 minutes, he should be able to get the ball into court while standing on the baseline.

THE STANCE

The stance of the beginner is the same as the stance of the advanced player. He does not face the net. His body is turned almost sideways, but not to the extent that he completely faces his own sideline. His feet are not in a line; the legs are spread 12 to 18 inches, with the left toe an inch behind the baseline and the left heel approximately six inches behind the baseline (the left foot is *not* parallel to the baseline). The right foot is a half step closer to the right alley than the left foot. The right foot is almost parallel to the baseline. This is the stance for serving in the forehand court. The right foot drops behind the left foot by half a step when serving into the backhand court.

The left foot may not touch the line nor may the right foot step into the court until the ball has been hit. The penalty for stepping on the line or into the court is a foot-fault.

THE GRIP

The beginner will hold his racket with a *forehand* grip. All advanced players serve with a backhand grip, but this will seem unnatural to a novice and will be very difficult for someone who has not had at least a year of racket experience. The serve should be smooth and flowing before the beginner attempts to use the backhand grip.

Dick Savitt has one of the most powerful serves in the game and he uses the compact wind-up. Frame one shows the start of the toss, with both racket and toss-arm up together. This is an excellent view of the shot-put type toss. The legs are apart and the weight is on the back foot. In Frame 2, Savitt arches his back and the racket comes down behind th back. The elbow is bent and the right foot is startin to come forward. Dick watches for footfaults and i a good two or three inches behind the line. I Frame 3, just before the hit, the arm is straight an Savitt has made full use of his height. The weigh

ELEMENTARY WIND-UP

Most novices will find it easier for the first few weeks or months to start the serve with the racket cocked over the right shoulder. This eliminates the wind-up temporarily, and it gives the player a chance to concentrate on toss, hit and follow-through. He starts his swing, therefore, with his right elbow jutting up, his right hand almost touching his right shoulder and the head of his racket "scratching" his back.

When the player is able to serve with reasonabl control with this shortened swing (after perhaps tw weeks to two months), it is time to add a wind-u to his stroke. The player has the choice of tw wind-ups—a small, compact one such as that use by Billy Talbert or Dick Savitt, or a wide, free swinging one, more commonly used by tournamen players. Both have their advantages. The small on seems to give the player more disguise; the bigge one enables the player to get full maximum swing

pes into the ball as the right foot swings forward. The wrist is straightening out by snapping forward; hence the velocity (speed) of the racket head is maximized. The fourth frame shows Savitt just after the hit. Note how much farther the racket head has moved than the arm due to the wrist snap forward.

The fifth frame shows the follow-through as the right leg swings over into court. It is practically a flat serve, with the wrist directing the ball. Savitt did not follow his serve to net. If he had, his body would have leaned further forward at this point and the right leg would have been farther in.

ng power. The beginner should choose the one to which he adapts most easily.

COMPACT WIND-UP

Both the small and the big wind-up are begun from the same position. The player stands slightly sideways to the net. The racket is held at waist-level, with the head perpendicular to the ground. The racket head, which is tilted up very slightly, points to the court in which the player is going to serve. The throat of the racket is cradled in the fingers of the left hand; it is not grasped tightly but lies gently on the finger tips. As the left hand rises with the toss, the right hand also moves straight up. It will bring the racket into the position previously described in the *Elementary Wind-Up*.

FULL WIND-UP

The starting position of the feet, racket and hands is the same as in the *Compact Wind-Up*. However, the right arm will take a full round-house

swing before reaching the "back-scratching" position just prior to the hit. At no point will the right arm stop or pause in its motion; it is all one continuous action. Arm and racket move in a semi-circle from the ready position, where the racket points in front of the body, to the end of the semi-circle, where the racket points to the bottom of the fence behind the player. In the ready position the elbow was bent, but as the semi-circle begins the arm straightens; and at the end of the semi-circle, the player's arm and racket are a straight line. They have moved some 150°, arm and racket now pointing downward behind the body. It is at this point that, without a pause, the player raises his racket to the back-scratching position. The whole action is one smooth, unhurried, continuous motion which should speed up perceptibly as the racket moves into the hit.

THE TOSS

The ball is held in the fingers of the left hand, never in the palm. The object is to *place* the ball in the air with complete accuracy. Therefore one does not throw from the palm but instead one places in the air with the fingers. Accuracy is obtained by releasing the ball at the last possible moment, which means when the left arm has straightened and is pointing directly upwards. As the right arm starts its wind-up, the left arm moves upward slowly until it is completely extended. Then the fingertips (thumb and first two fingers) shot-put the ball upward. In the full wind-up the right arm must travel much farther than the left. Both arms start their motions at the same time, and the left arm will therefore have to move more slowly so that there will be no pause at any time in the action.

The object is to place the ball about 6" to the right of and 12" in front of the body—to the right because this enables the player to put spin on the serve, and to the front so that the players's weight can move into the ball. The toss should be high enough so that the server can hit it on the center of the racket when arm and racket are fully extended. If the beginner can achieve a perfect toss, the rest of the service action becomes relatively simple. He should therefore practice it two or three hours or until the toss is absolutely accurate. It will solve most of his service problems.

46

All top serves show a similar action at the end toss. Compare this picture of Margaret Smith wi of Mike Sangster (on the previous page) and Neale (on the facing page). Margaret has brought her r too far forward for this stage of the serve; her may shift into the court before the hit.

Fraser is shown at a slightly later stage of his great left-handed serve. The racket is on its way down his back. This is a full, free, uninhibited action, ugh Neale were brandishing a whip rather than a He can snap the racket with as much wrist.

THE HIT

From the back-scratching position, the racket and arm move upward until they form an almost straight line. The racket trails slightly behind the wrist since the object is to hit the ball with a wrist snap. At the moment of impact, which takes place slightly to the right and a little in front of the body, the arm and racket are a straight line.

WEIGHT TRANSFER

When the server stands in the ready position, his weight is equally distributed on both feet. As his arms start the service motion, the weight moves to the right foot; the left shoulder moves up and the right shoulder moves down. The right knee is straight and the left knee is slightly bent. In other words, the body is tilted back, so that at the moment of the hit it can move forward into the ball. The body is a straight line as the ball is struck. The right shoulder moves forward into the court on the follow-through.

FOLLOW-THROUGH

The arm and racket are a straight line at the moment of impact. The racket head leads slightly on the follow-through because of the wrist snap, while arm and racket sweep through the ball and across the left leg without a pause. The right shoulder has also followed through, and it points downward over the left foot.

Beginners should never follow their serves into net; intermediates should do so only in doubles. The advanced player will always come in behind his serve in doubles and will frequently do so in singles. When the player is coming to net, his right foot will step into the court immediately after the service hit.

SLICE, TWIST AND FLAT SERVE

The *slice* is the basic delivery for all players, whether beginners or advanced. The racket face sweeps across the side of the ball farthest from the body instead of striking it directly from behind.

The perfect *flat serve*, on the other hand, has almost no spin and no chance of going in if the player is less than six feet tall. The flat serve moves in a straight line from the middle of the racket face down to the court, but in the process it must clear the net. The very tall player, therefore, can hit flat serves, but others must utilize spin to give the ball a curved trajectory.

Slice is the easiest to impart and the least wearing on the server. Heavy slice will "bite"—*i.e.*, take off sideways. Beginners need light or medium slice for control, although the advanced player will frequently use heavy slice for change of pace.

The *American twist* is only good if it is served well. Otherwise it will provide an easy set-up for the receiver. It must be deep and it must have a high kick to the backhand side. *Twist* is put on the ball by tossing it slightly behind the head (instead of in front and to the right as in the slice serve), then bringing the racket face across the ball from left to right. The right arm follows through past the right leg. It demands a great amount of back action since the bend is from the small of the back.

YOUR GOAL

The server is given two chances to get the ball into court. There is no point in throwing away the first chance with a hard ball that never goes in. The first serve should go into court *at least 70% of the time.* The touring pros will occasionally get in 80% or 90%. If the first ball is a fault, the second serve should *always* go in. Double-faults are suicidal; there is no reason to give the opponent a "free" point. The second serve should therefore be hit with enough spin to go in, with sufficient pace and placement to prevent the opponent from murdering it, and with 100% accuracy. It cannot be a "push," and so the player should practice until he has a reliable second serve.

A serve (first or second) should have excellent depth and should be placed most of the time to the backhand. Even when an opponent's backhand is better than his forehand, he will almost invariably make a more forceful return off the forehand. In singles, one serves to the forehand only to catch a player off balance.

THE SERVE: SINGLES AND DOUBLES

The proper position for serving in the forehand court in singles is immediately to the right of the center service line. In doubles, the correct position is half-way between the center service line and the alley *or* closer to the alley. Some players serve from two feet inside the alley line. The server stands near the center in singles to avoid leaving more than half the backhand court open. In doubles, the server has more leeway, although most will choose to play from a spot between two and six feet from the alley line.

The position is entirely different when the player is serving in singles into the backhand court. Now he can either stand just to the left of the center service line or between two and four feet to the left of the center service line (provided he is not coming to net). He will be serving to the backhand almost exclusively, and few of his opponent's backhand returns can be belted down the line out of

his forehand reach. If the server has a reliable del(ery) to the backhand and a pretty good forehand, can stand as much as four feet to the left of t center service line. In doubles, the server star two feet inside the alley line so that he can se wide to the backhand. He follows his serve into at an angle.

CORRECTING SERVICE FLAWS

Check yourself on these common errors:

Insufficient spin. The toss and the grip determi the spin. Heavy spin can be imparted to the b by throwing it well to the right of and slightly front of the body. It is very difficult to get go spin with a forehand grip. Check to make sure th the grip is not slipping over to the forehand duri the wind-up. Make sure that the racket face me the ball on the side farthest from the body.

Insufficient power. This can be caused by a p toss (not far enough in front of the body), lack wrist snap or weight moving backwards rather th forwards. The toss should never be directly ov the head except in the case of an American twi A good serve must have wrist action, and this easiest to achieve with a backhand grip. T beginner's greatest problem will occur in achi ing the proper weight shift: the grip, toss a hit may be good, but the weight is not coming f ward. This is worst when the player ends by ber ing at the waist, having left hips completely of action. A corrective measure is to concentra on transferring weight from right foot to left a on moving the hips into the court.

Too much slice. The server can correct this fect, which is causing the ball to go wide of t service court, by flattening the face of his rack slightly. Too much bevel to the right causes cessive spin, and so the server must turn his wr (and racket) leftwards while still maintaining t backhand grip. This will feel awkward and natural to the beginner, but a half-hour of pract will restore his "feel" for the serve. Do not corr by going back to the forehand grip.

Too low or too high a toss. When the toss is t low, the player loses all the advantage of his heig and of hitting down on the ball. He can get s but not power. If the toss is too high, the ball weave with the wind as the player waits for it descend. Too lofty a toss often disrupts the smoo ness of the wind-up, for the player has to pa while he waits for the ball to come down to proper level.

Rocking. Many beginners "bow" as they preparing to toss. As the left arm comes do the novice rocks forward instead of shifting weight backwards. He can correct this failing not allowing the left arm to drop below waist le

ad by standing with his full weight on the right
ot. Nothing is added to a serve by allowing the
ft hand to drop. It will take full concentration on
e movements of the left arm to cure this fault,
id it should be done before the "bowing" becomes
habit.

No body action. In the attempt to prevent the
eight from moving backward at the hit, some
ayers will overcorrect and hold the body stiff
roughout the action. This is far better than
ocking," since it is easy to add body action where
ere has been none before. The player should try

to start the serve with his left shoulder higher than
his right. As he hits, he should concentrate on
putting his right shoulder and body behind the impact and on throwing his right shoulder and body
into the court with the follow-through.

Pushing. A weak pat-ball delivery is developed
through fear of serving a double-fault. The easiest
way to correct is to learn a spin serve, then practice
hitting it as hard as possible. Defects are corrected
by overexaggeration of the opposite trait, and several weeks of walloping the ball with spin will help
to develop a feel for power play.

SUMMARY

1. The beginner's grip is the forehand; the ad-
nced grip is the backhand.

2. In the ready position, the body is almost side-
ays to the net and the feet are 12 to 18 inches
part and not in a line.

3. Arms are at waist level as the action starts.
he racket throat is cradled in the fingers of the
ft hand and the racket head points to the court
which the player is serving.

4. Weight is on the back (right) foot. It shifts to
e front (left) foot with the hit.

5. The ball is held lightly in the fingers of the
ft hand; it is not released until the left arm is
lly extended.

6. The toss is to a point 6" to the right of, and
" in front of, the body for the slice serve.

7. In the *compact wind-up*, the right arm rises
rectly from the ready position to the back-scratch-
g action.

8. In the *full wind-up*, the right arm sweeps
wn and backward in a semi-circle, then rises
thout pause to the back-scratching position. The
tion speeds up toward the end.

9. Ball is hit at the top of the toss. Right arm

and racket are a straight line at the moment of
impact.

10. Racket head trails behind the wrist just before the hit so that the ball can be struck with wrist
action.

11. Right shoulder and hips follow through into
the court. Right arm swings down past the left leg
in the flat or slice action.

12. Right foot steps into the court when the
player is following his serve into net.

13. The first serve should go into the court at
least 70% of the time; the second serve should always go in.

14. Try for consistency, then accuracy, then
power.

15. In singles, stand close to the center service
line when serving in the forehand court but op-
tionally two to four feet to the left of the center
service line when serving in the backhand court.

16. In doubles, stand in the middle of the forehand service court or to the right of this point.
When serving to the backhand court in doubles, the
player may stand two feet inside the alley line.

17. Almost all serves in singles should be directed
to the backhand.

Lefty Neale Fraser illustrates how far forward the net rusher tosses the ball and how careful one should be in planting the front foot to make sure it is behind the line. Fraser allows two or three inches. This action is somewhat different from Savitt's (page 44). Fraser's left elbow (racket arm) is close to the body; Savitt brings his back farther. The ball is still going up

This is the perfect back-scratching action. Fra though arched, is leaning far forward and his le swinging over. He could hit flat, slice or kick (Amer twist) from this same stance and wind-up action varying his wrist motion. He has power from his thrust as well as from wrist action.

ck McKinley, although not as tall as great servers
 Fraser, has a similar action and makes full use of
height and power. He also can vary his service spins
ill, but because he is not as tall he must put more
 on his second ball to make sure he brings it into
t. The toss to his left and his arched back are
cative of an American twist.

Lew Hoad has also arched his back and you can tell
he too is hitting an American twist by the toss to his
left. His right foot is coming forward and he is going
to attack (come to net) behind his serve. Note that the
toss is about 18 inches to the left of Hoad's left foot.
As with all good serves, the arm is straight at the
moment of impact.

51

CHAPTER 10

How To Hit
The Overhead

The overhead—a stroke made above head heigh
—is a kind of abbreviated serve. It is also called
"smash." The left (toss) arm has no function, an
the action of the right arm is usually much le
pronounced ("smaller") than in the service. Th
player simply picks up his right arm, lets th
racket head drop behind the back, straightens th
arm so it points upward, then hits the ball with
pronounced wrist snap.

There are several prerequisites to a good overhea
The body's left side is to the net, the racket is he
with a backhand grip and the feet are comfortab
apart. The ball is hit either with no spin at a
(when the player is closer in than the service lin
or with a small amount of slice (when the play
is hitting from the back court). The player mu
move toward the ball. Therefore his feet shou
not be planted until the hit begins. This enabl
him to be flexible if the ball should waver in th
air. The ball should be taken at the point where
will meet the center of the racket when the arm an
racket are perfectly extended; if the lob is not th
high, the ball should be taken as a high volley.
the ball is misjudged and the player has to hit
when it is low, he bends his knees. (Quite a fe
men with powerful overheads will almost kneel
hit a low ball as an overhead rather than as
volley.)

TIMING

There is only one way to learn an overhead—
practice. After the stance and hit are memorize
the player must acquire proper timing. If the b
ginner has a serious problem in acquiring a r
liable smash, the easiest and quickest method
acquire timing is by using a paddle rather than
racket. He will be able to time the ball immediatel
Within an hour, he can switch back to the full-size
racket and he will usually find that he now has
good swing and a much better eye.

The overhead must be absolutely grooved. N
player can ever come to net if his opponents ca
successfully lob against him. The lob must b
looked upon as the "set-up" for which the net ma
has been waiting. Occasionally the lob will cato
the net man wrong-footed; sometimes the lob w
be just a few inches too high and force the volley
into error. Often the lob will be so deep that th
net man will have to run back to the baseline
retrieve it. More commonly, the lob will be le
than perfect, and it must then be put away by th
smasher.

Pierre Darmon is jumping for an overhead from behind the service line, so it must have been a good lob.
with the serve, all good jump overheads show similarity, a scissors kick of the legs being the hallmar
Darmon has turned the racket face out to guide the smash to his right, which is the action most top playe
prefer on this shot. The left arm is in a peculiar position, but this crossed arm shows up in many smash phot
and is probably a natural balancing action.

Bob Hewitt of Australia hits an overhead. The ball is on the racket; the racket and arm are a straight line, but the wrist is snapping the racket's head forward. The lob was a good one; it necessitated a jump from behind the service line.

CONSISTENCY IS ALL

The qualities of a good overhead are consistenc placement and pace. Consistency is the most in portant since speed counts for nothing if the ba does not go in. Overheads must be thoughtfull placed, since a good retriever can throw them ba all day if they are within his reach. Pace is th final characteristic of a good overhead, since the are many occasions when speed and surprise a required to put the ball away.

The most difficult lob to return is a high, de ball. It must be taken in the back court, since it descending rapidly. As an alternative, it must be k from a position well behind the baseline after t ball has bounced. The farther back the smash stands, the harder it is for him to put away t ball. In any case, the smash must be retrieved wi a fair amount of slice to keep the ball in court; t farther back the ball is taken, the more slice mu be used. Deep overheads should be placed, not k for winners.

SUMMARY

1. Left side to net, feet wide apart
2. Roundhouse backswing eliminated
3. Racket held with backhand grip
4. Racket brought straight up, then racket hea "scratches" player's back
5. Ball taken when racket and arm are a straig line
6. Feet not planted until hit begins
7. Wrist snaps forward at moment of impact
8. Short overheads are hit flat
9. Deep overheads are hit with slice
10. Emphasis on consistency and placement, the on power

Fred Stolle had to jump from behind th line to bring down this lob. He displays th scissors kick; his left arm is held in close.

Chuck McKinley, short but powerful, agile and fast, is one of the most acrobatic players in the game. It i
very difficult to get a lob over his head. Here at Wimbledon he has had to jump high and in a hurry, so th
scissors kick is missing, but he has had time to control the direction of the ball with his wrist.

Like Sangster, when he can, stays on the ground on his overhead—just as McKinley jumps by preference. While Sangster's left foot remains planted, his right leg is out in front in a scissors-like action for balance. Sangster's wrist has snapped forward as he has hit the shot, similar to the action on the serve.

How To

Lob

CHAPTER 11

HOW TO HIT THE LOB

The lob is a groundstroke in which the ball
hit up into the air, the object being to lift the ba
over the opponent's head. It is hit with the sam
grip and foot work as the backhand and foreha
groundstrokes. However, in order to loft the ba
over the net man, the racket face must be ope
The backswing is the same, but the tilt of th
racket and the follow-through are different fro
that of the groundstrokes.

THE DEFENSIVE LOB

There are two kinds of lobs—the defensive an
the offensive. The former is used to get the play
out of trouble. The ball is sent high into the ai
well out of the reach of the net man, and it lan
in the area of the baseline. The defensive lob
used not only when the player is in a bad positic
and his opponent is at net but also when the opp
nent is *on the baseline*. Then, because the ball
sailing high and deep, the player has a chance
return to the center of the court. From what ma
have been a hopeless position, he is back in th
point again.

The key to the defensive lob is height and dept
The ball should be hit either flat or with backsp
(it is difficult to control the hit of a high ball wi
much overspin). Where backspin is used, the rack
face is open and the motion of arm and racket
forward but only slightly upward. When the ball
hit flat (or with slight overspin), the racket face
almost completely open and the motion is almo
straight up in the air.

THE OFFENSIVE LOB

This lob is designed to catch the opponent o
balance. Its basis is disguise, for, if the oppone
sees it coming, he only needs to take a few ste
backward and smash the ball away. The shot is n

high as the defensive lob: it clears the extended racket of the net man by a safe margin but it is not sky-ball. The best offensive lob will bounce with forward motion, *i.e.*, toward the opponent's fence. Therefore it should be hit with topspin.

The racket face is half open—at about a 45° angle and the racket travels upward at about a 45° angle also. The trajectory should just clear the net man's jump reach, land deep in his court and bounce forward from the topspin. Offensive lobs with backspin can be made to clear the net man but their bounce will not carry forward, of course. This means the net man may run them down on the bounce.

The *defensive lob* is used more often in singles than doubles, although Italian stars Lea Pericoli and Sylvana Lazzarino have been phenomenally successful in using it against most top opposition. The *offensive lob* is used equally in singles and doubles. In singles it is a passing shot; in doubles, it is a passing shot and a method of taking the net away from the opposition. Even the tallest men with the biggest overheads can be caught wrong-footed by a well-disguised offensive lob. In doubles, the partner of the lobbed man may be able to retrieve it but the lobber and his partner can use the opportunity to take the net.

LOBBING TIPS

Lob over the backhand.

In singles, lob to keep the opponent from crowding the net.

In doubles, use the offensive lob to the server's partner as an alternate return of serve.

When lobbing defensively, remember the length of the court from baseline to baseline is 78 feet; make sure your lob goes the full distance.

• When in doubt, choose the defensive in preference to the offensive lob.

• When lobbing offensively in doubles, be sure to clear the extended racket of the net man; a poor offensive lob usually means immediate loss of the point.

• An offensive lob has no value if it is not disguised.

• When you are in trouble, the defensive lob is the safest shot.

• In singles, lob frequently (both defensively and offensively) against a net-rusher.

• Learn to lob offensively and defensively on both forehand and backhand.

• Hit harder and higher when lobbing against the wind; use more backspin or overspin when lobbing with the wind.

IMPROVING YOUR LOB

Ask a friend to help you by counting the number and variety of your lobs in the course of a match.

They should be tabulated as follows:

1. *Forehand offensive lobs*
   a) The number you hit per set;
   b) The number of outright winners;
   c) The number of errors you made through 1) ball falling short and 2) landing beyond the court area;
   d) the number of lobs your opponent reached;
   e) The number of points you won and lost on these lobs.

2. *Backhand offensive lobs*
   Same tabulations.

3. *Forehand defensive lobs*
   a) The number you hit per set;
   b) The number of points you "saved" by lobbing from a bad position;
   c) The number of errors you made through 1) ball falling short and 2) landing outside the court boundaries;
   d) The number of lobs your opponent put away;
   e) The number of points you won and lost on these lobs.

4. *Backhand defensive lobs*
   Same tabulations.

The resultant record will show you which lobs have been the most effective and where your lobbing weaknesses lie. The top pros not only lob far more than the amateurs, but they also lob defensively far more than offensively.

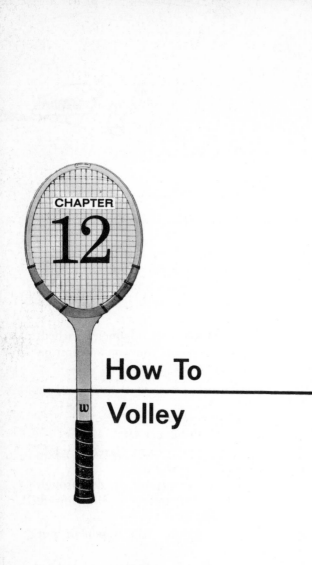

CHAPTER 12

How To
Volley

Dennis Ralston is just inside the service line in the center of the court, following through on a backhand volley down the center, perhaps to cut down Frank Froehling's potential angle. The racket head finishes low on an underspin volley. Note Froehling's excellent ready position.

The word *volley* means the flight of the tennis
ball or its course before striking the ground. A
"volley" is also a return of the ball before it touches
the ground.

Every player, sooner or later, finds himself in a
fast exchange with no time to change to forehand
or backhand, and therefore the same grip must be
used on both sides. This grip, which can be called
the Continental or the Eastern backhand, should
be learned as soon as possible. A beginner may
prefer to use the Eastern forehand grip until he
gets the feel of racket meeting ball, but he should
be encouraged to switch to the Continental when
he gets his timing and when his wrist becomes
strong enough. (*See page 13.*)

The proper position for the volley is halfway
between the service line and the net. The player
faces his opponent with his feet 18 inches apart,
his knees slightly flexed and the racket in front of
him with the throat cradled in the left hand. He
will not stroke the ball; he will punch it. There is
no backswing as in a groundstroke. The volley
starts just at the side of the body and it very much
resembles a boxing jab.

STEP INTO IT

The beginner should step toward the ball just
before the hit. If the ball is coming to his forehand,
he steps forward and sideways with his left foot.
If the ball is too far from his forehand to reach
comfortably, he must lunge forward, stretching as
wide as he can, preferably with the left foot moving
both forward and sideways. The more advanced
player can step sideways and forward with his right
foot, but this may create a problem with balance
for the beginner.

On the backhand, the player steps forward (and
sideways) with his right foot. Only the advanced
player, who has no problems with balance, can step
sideways or forward with the left foot.

Readiness, balance and a short punch are keys to
a good volley. The player must be far more alert
than he is in the back court since he has far less
time to prepare for the shot. If he is not ready, he
will not be able to step forward and hit the volley
well in front of him. If the player is off balance, his
weight will move away from the ball instead of
toward it and the shot will lack pace. If the volley
is a drive instead of a short punch, the player loses
precision and control.

Butch Bucholz breaks his wrist to control a forehand low volley inside the service line. Note the
open face to bring the ball up and impart backspin.
Butch has a hammer grip—fingers are close together
rather than spread. This is a fine example of the
Continental volley.

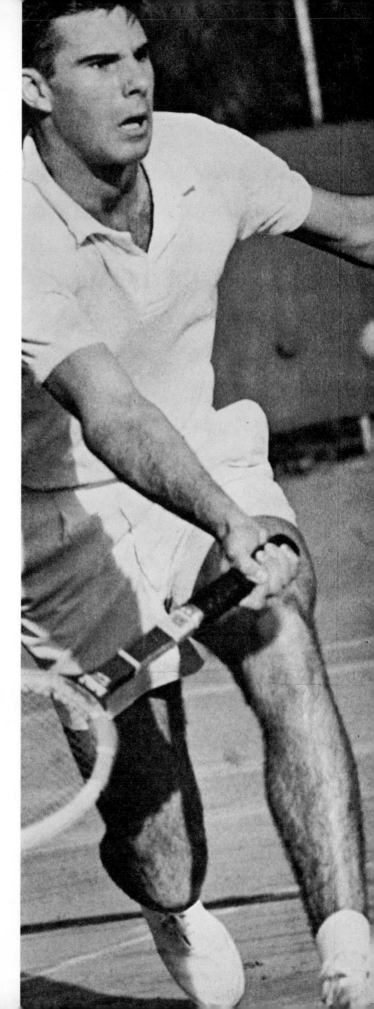

Lew Hoad starts to his right for a fore-hand volley, racket cradled in his left hand.

His eye on the ball, he p[...] right foot, starts to draw h[...] back.

BEND THE KNEES

When the player steps forward in anticipation [...] the ball, all his weight moves forward as well. T[...] beginner's tendency is to step forward but to be[...] from the waist, which means the hips (and weigh[...] have lagged behind. To correct this tendency, t[...] back should be absolutely straight at all times; t[...] only bend is from the knees. Many good volleye[...] have a rigid back, but the knees will almost tou[...] the ground on low shots.

The racket *head* is always tilted upwards exce[...] on balls below net level. On high volleys, the rack[...]

Racket head remains above wrist through-out stroke and racket face is almost flat.

The hit is almost flat an[...] front of body. On low vo[...] hits with underspin.

spread as he completes his motion. Note the short wind-volley.

Moving into the ball, his wind-up is complete and he will get power from forward body motion.

Left leg comes forward as body pivots, bringing racket toward ball with very little arm motion.

almost perpendicular to the ground. On volleys above net level, the racket head tilts upward y slightly. On low balls below net level, the ket head is parallel to the ground. The racket d never points downward since one can only op the ball *upwards* from such a position, and s puts the volleyer in a very bad spot.

On high volleys, the player should punch through ball in a downward direction. The *face* of the ket is therefore almost flat (perpendicular to the und) since the player can hit hard and still clear net without resort to excessive spin.

On volleys that are only slightly above net level, the racket face must "open" (tilt backward slightly) so that underspin is imparted to the ball. If the player hits down (with a flat face) on these balls, they would not clear the net or they would fall short.

On volleys that are below net level, the player must open the racket face so that it is tilting very much toward the sky—the only way to clear the net. Additionally, there must a *forward* motion (a short punch) to carry the ball deep into the opponent's court.

es the ball with his wrist. s shifted to left foot, which anted.

A long follow-through is possible only on a high volley. This is a stroke volley.

This is only window dressing. It is too long a follow-through for any volley except a kill.

Chuck McKinley is completely stretched out for this forehand stop volley, but his balance is good and he has the ball on the center of the racket with a firm wrist. He is hitting with right foot forward, but he is leaping for the ball, only his balance—not ~~~ foot is forward—counts.

ESSENTIALS OF THE VOLLEY

Reviewing the essential ingredients of the good volley:

- readiness, balance and short punch;
- racket head pointing upwards (on high balls) or sideways (on very low balls);
- racket face that is almost flat (on high balls), slightly open (on shoulder-height balls) and very open (on low balls);
- back always straight but knees that bend on waist-high or low balls.

The beginner *should never bend his wrist* on a volley unless he is hitting a very high ball. The mark of a great volley is a stiff wrist. A wrist as strong as steel moves the ball; the ball, which can be moving very fast, never moves the wrist. Power comes from shoulder, forearm (between elbow and hand), and body weight moving forward. The wrist is locked and does not snap or bend at all. The position of the wrist is the same at the end of the volley as it is at the beginning.

A single exception: On a very high volley wrist can snap forward as it does on the serve overhead.

ARM AND WRIST

The position of the arm and wrist is slightly ferent on the forehand volley than it is on the b hand. On the forehand, the arm is slightly l except when stretching wide for a ball. The wri laid back slightly. The shoulder and entire move forward in a punch motion, and at the fi the arm is either straight or almost straight an points in the general area of the opponent's fe On the backhand, the racket and forearm form most a straight line (the wrist is not laid ba There is a comfortable bend in the elbow, again the hit is from shoulder and forearm. arm comes close to straightening at the finish points in the general direction of the oppone fence.

Both in singles and doubles the net man m be prepared to move—to his left, to his right,

64

d to take the advantage, backward to cover a
. The ball seldom comes right to the volleyer.
e beginner, however, must first learn to handle
ls that come to him before attempting to move
le to the left or the right. He must learn to
idle high, medium and low volleys. If he starts
h the proper stroke he will enjoy playing net
nediately and will improve rapidly.

PRACTICING THE VOLLEY

n the elementary stages, his practice opponent or
coach should hit high, soft balls to him to help
1 get the feeling of moving into the ball. If his
ponent hits too hard, he will not be ready, he
l take the ball late and he will back up.

Gradually he will learn to open the racket face
medium-high balls and to open it up even more
low balls. His returns should be aimed for *con-
ency,* not for power or placement.

When he is able to return 20 soft balls consecu-
ely, he can try for *control.* Control means depth
l placement. The net man now tries to return
h ball deep to the center. If his balls are going
far to the right, he should overcorrect by hitting
far to the left. Consistency, depth and accuracy
cede power and touch.

Margaret Smith is close to net for a low backhand volley, which she hits with a stiff, cocked wrist, giving plenty of underspin to the ball. Knees are bent to get down to the ball for she, like Hoad, never bends above the hips. A good volley is as important in women's play as in men's.

The beginner should stand at net for at least 10 minutes of every practice session. Each time he should review the fundamentals so that the basic stroke becomes grooved and so that he avoids forming bad habits.

To summarize:

1. The player stands halfway between the service line and the net in the center of the court.

2. His feet are 18 inches apart, his knees are slightly flexed and his racket points in front of him, with the throat cradled in the fingers of the left hand.

3. His grip is the Continental (he uses the Eastern forehand only in the beginning stages).

4. Just before the ball comes to him, he steps forward—with the left foot for forehand volleys and with the right foot for backhand volleys.

5. If the ball comes wide, he steps forward and sideways.

6. His back is always straight; if the ball is low, he bends his knees.

7. The racket head points upwards on high balls, slightly upwards on balls above waist level, and sideways on low balls.

8. The racket face is almost flat on very high volleys, slightly open on shoulder-high volleys and wide open on low volleys.

9. The volley is a punch rather than a stroke; the racket starts by the body and moves forward toward the ball.

10. The wrist remains rigid on all but touch shots.

11. On the forehand volley, the arm is bent (except for wide balls) and the wrist is laid back slightly.

12. On the backhand volley, the arm is bent but the wrist is not laid back.

13. All volleys end with the arm almost straigh[t] it points in the general direction of the opponen[t's] fence.

The learner should try first for consistency, the[n] for depth and placement. When the ball com[es] directly at him as the net man, he should alwa[ys] take it on the backhand. It is impossible to take [a] ball that comes right at you on the forehand. [As] the player develops more confidence, his practi[ce] opponent or his coach can hit the ball harder [at] him. If he starts backing away or taking the ba[ll] late, he should go back to returning soft ball[s.] When he is able to hit balls well that come to hi[m,] he can start moving toward balls that are hit aw[ay] from him. He should forget about power, angl[e] and touch shots until he has mastered moving f[or] wide balls and returning them with consistency a[nd] depth.

WHEN TO PLAY NET

Although the beginner *practices* his volley eve[ry] time he steps on the court, he should come to n[et] only on a special occasion when he *plays*. H[e] should *never* come in on his serve in singles becau[se] he has not yet learned to serve forcefully to h[is] opponent's backhand. He should *always* come [in] on any ball that is hit inside the service line *if* [he] can hit the proper approach shot. He should h[it] the short ball as deep as he can to his opponen[t's] backhand and he should then move *toward th[e] opponent's backhand area* to anticipate the retur[n.] If the beginner is not capable of hitting deep to [the] backhand, he is not yet ready to take the net agai[nst] an opponent. The most elementary tactic of volle[y] ing is based on a good approach shot (one that go[es] deep to the opponent's backhand).

The beginner will do most of his volleying in doubles rather than singles. Here he need not have acquired an approach shot, since he can take the volleying position whenever his partner is serving. He stands at net ready to move forward and to either side. He must be far more alert than he is in the back court since he has far less time to get ready for the ball. He should try to cover only a small area of the net. No beginner is ready to "poach" (run across the net to cut off a wide return). Even in practice matches the novice must not try shots he has not yet learned. Elementary tactics are as important for the beginner as advanced tactics are for the champion, and just as the expert will not try a difficult shot when a simple one will suffice, so the learner must never attempt a style of play which will result in too many errors.

The intermediate (not the beginner) can try to come in on his serve in doubles. If he misses more than half his volleys, he should not attempt to come in on his serve any more. The object of the game is to get the ball in court, not to miss by trying advanced plays. The intermediate should always stand at net when his partner serves, and here he will get plenty of opportunities to test his volley.

The advanced player always comes in on his serve in doubles. He only comes in on his serve in singles on a very fast surface or against an opponent who is returning his serve high and short.

To conclude, it is one thing to learn the strokes; it is another thing to learn when to use them. The volley is practiced regularly by the beginner but is used only rarely by him when he plays a match.

The *drop shot* is a stroke with volley action in which the player endeavors to make the ball barely drop over the net and then die.

Arthur Ashe is a talented young player who has all the equipment to become a champion. His forehand volley is either a winner or an error since he hits it very hard and close to the lines. When he stretches and gets down to the ball, as he is doing here, and when he holds his wrist stiff on the punch, again as here, his accuracy increases. Note that the racket head is well above wrist level.

Learning
The Drop Shot And Drop Volley

The drop shot is not a stroke for the elementa or intermediate player. It is not vital for the a vanced player nor is it an absolute necessity for t champion. However, it is a shot that gives a play an additional advantage *if* he can execute it pr erly and *if* he uses it at the proper time. A play who learns it has acquired a knowledge of wr movement, and this knowledge will help him lea the angle game and all the touch shots. He w find the drop shot invaluable against the sl player or the man who hates to come to net; he w rarely find it useful against a fast, attacki opponent.

You never hit a drop shot from the back court when your opponent is on the service line. You not drop shot a good opponent in the latter sta of the match. Use the drop shot sparingly exce against opponents who are clumsy, slow or ve tired.

The drop shot is used for change of pace, to cat an opponent off balance or to keep him from g ting grooved. It must have disguise to be of val

Most important of all, the drop shot must cle the net and it must bounce short and low. If bounces high, it is almost a sure winner for t opponent.

HOW TO DROP SHOT

The drop shot is hit with underspin. The rack face must be open and the racket must move in downward direction as it contacts the ball. T action of the racket is both down and forward. T brushing of the racket under the ball makes rotate backward; when the ball clears the net, bounces low or even backward.

The drop shot can be an outright winner wh the opponent is out of positon or caught movi the wrong way. Frequently the opponent can g to the drop shot but can do little with it. T means he is in a perfect position to be trapped a lob. The drop shot-and-lob sequence, if vari with deep drives, can wear down all but t strongest opposition.

Drop shots can be very effective against we second serves. The drop shotter will invariably fi plenty of opportunities against a non-aggressi

ayer. He will have far fewer chances against the
~wer server and net rusher, but even the latter
~ll occasionally supply the drop shotter with
portunities.

Not every good player uses the drop shot but
~ery good player learns the reply to it. He must
~ther drop shot back (it must be a perfect drop
~ot since his opponent is on or inside the service
~e), angle the ball sharply or hit deep to his
ponent's baseline. He must *never hit short,* for
is provides the opposition with the perfect set-up.

THE DROP VOLLEY

Every good net man has acquired a drop volley.
~e uses it infrequently or often, depending on his
~ill in its execution. Here he is right on top of the
~t, not merely inside or on the service line, and
~erefore the drop volley will be even more effec-
~ve than the drop shot. It is used, obviously, when
~e opponent is on the baseline or out of position
~ moving in the wrong direction. It carries its own
~sguise, since the action of the drop volley is only
~vealed when the ball is hit.

The drop volley is executed by coming more
~arply under the ball or by pulling the arm back
~st at the moment of impact. At the last moment
~e wrist turns under. It is not an easily acquired
~ot; advanced players who have difficulty learning
~ should concentrate on the sharply angled volley,
~hich is just as effective.

Camouflage the dropshot for surprise

69

CHAPTER

14

How To Play
The Half-Volley

The half-volley is a stroke never used by beg
ners, seldom used by intermediates and frequen
used by advanced players. It is not a volley, sin
the ball has already bounced. It is primarily
"block" stroke. The half-volley is used to retu
balls that have bounced at the player's feet. T
ball is picked up on the racket immediately af
the bounce, often when it has risen only six
eight inches from the ground. If the ball boun
two feet high, it is no longer a half-volley; it
either a forehand or a backhand stroke.

Under no circumstances should a beginner e
hit a half-volley. The first-year tennist moves seve
steps back when a deep ball is coming to av
having to half-volley. The intermediate player u
this stroke only when coming in on his serve
doubles. Occasionally he may not get in on
delivery fast enough, and the return will bounce
his feet. The advanced player will have to ha
volley frequently since he attacks in singles, a
a good return of serve may catch him in the a
just behind the service line.

If a volleyer finds himself half-volleying often
shots other than the "first volley," he should co
in closer. He is definitely too far back and is losi
opportunities to make angle volley placeme
from close in. He must take more chances a
occasionally be lobbed over; it will pay off.

The intermediate player learns the half-vol
but tries to hit it as seldom as possible. There
occasions when he must use it, but he should
whenever possible to hit either a ground-stroke
a volley in preference. He can use either a foreha
or a volley grip on the forehand half-volley. This
strictly a matter of personal preference, althou
the champions who half-volley frequently find t
Continental or volley grip is more satisfacto
Whatever the grip, the ball must be hit with
underspin. It is difficult enough to make an aggr
sive half-volley, and underspin only slows up t
ball and causes it to soar.

HITTING THE HALF-VOLLEY

A short wind-up is vital; a long wind-up wou
destroy the accuracy on a hurried stroke. If there
time for a complete wind-up, then one has ti
to move into position for a proper forehand
backhand or to move forward to volley. By defi
tion, a half-volley is hit close to the ground. The
fore a player must *get down* to the ball. The m
common error is to stand straight and allow t
arm and racket head to drop. This makes for
shovel rather than a stroke. The legs should
spread and the knees bent, with the racket he
parallel to the ground or only slightly angled dow

WHERE TO TAKE THE BALL

The half-volley should be taken in front of the [pla]yer, who is stretching forward. If he is trapped [so] that he has to take the ball by his side or behind [hi]m (this can happen on the volley following return [of] serve), a Continental or volley grip is best be-[cau]se it permits easier wrist action to direct the [ba]ll into the court.

When a half-volley is hit from the baseline, it [mu]st have a follow-through to provide depth and [so]me pace; otherwise it will set up in mid-court. [Th]e wind-up, however, is still short. When a half-[vo]lley is hit from mid-court or closer to the net, it [ca]nnot have much follow-through because the ball [wi]ll sail out of court.

It is extremely difficult to use spin control on [th]e half-volley. An occasional player such as [W]hitney Reed can put topspin on a half-volley. [Ot]her players such as Manuel Santana or Ken Rose-[wa]ll can make backspin dropshots out of half-[vol]leys. But these cannot be part of the repertoire [of] any but the most naturally talented champions.

Direction and placement are not difficult if the player pays attention to detail and is prepared, but depth control is difficult because only a little spin can be used. Short half-volleys create the biggest problem because they give the opponent an opportunity to attack. If the half-volley can be hit deep, the player is in a much better position to handle the next return.

Half-volleys should be hit from the baseline only rarely. If the player finds himself hitting too many half-volleys from the backcourt, something is wrong. Either his opponent is hitting superbly and every ball is landing right on or near the baseline, or the player himself is standing too far in. In either case he should back up so that he can get a better hit at the ball.

In conclusion, the half-volley is generally a mid-court shot, used by a player who is advancing to net and who is trapped in this area by a fine return of serve. The only time you half-volley from the baseline is when you are caught by a particularly good return from an attacking, aggressive opponent.

[M]arty Riessen is trapped on the service line, which often happens to players coming to net behind their [se]rve. He plays a backhand half-volley with a firm wrist and a very short stroke. Marty is well down to the [ba]ll and has not dropped the racket head, which is nicely parallel to the ground. It is preferable to take the [ba]ll more in front of the body.

Your
Return-Of-Serve

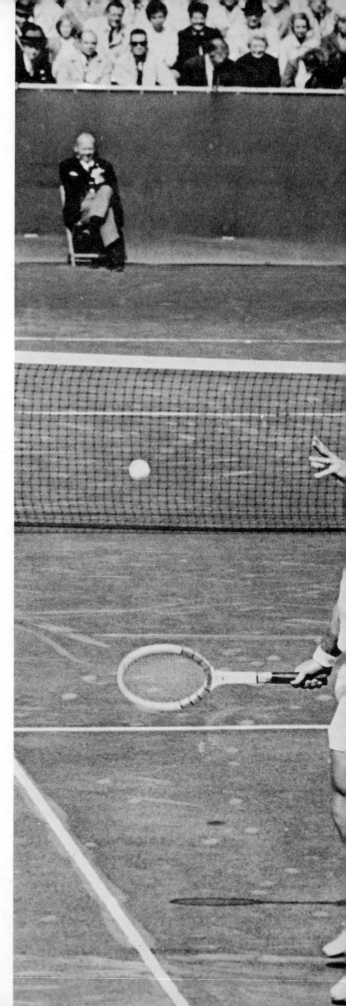

Chuck McKinley (in the foreground) is blocking a backhand return-of-serve to Fred Stolle. Chuck is standing inside the baseline on slow clay for two reasons: If Stolle serves wide to his backhand, McKinley can take the ball before it pulls him too wide; and more important, if Stolle comes to net behind serve, the closer McKinley is, the more chance he has of hurting Stolle by making him volley up. Stolle chose not to come in on this shot. Very few players can do so successfully on clay on second serves.

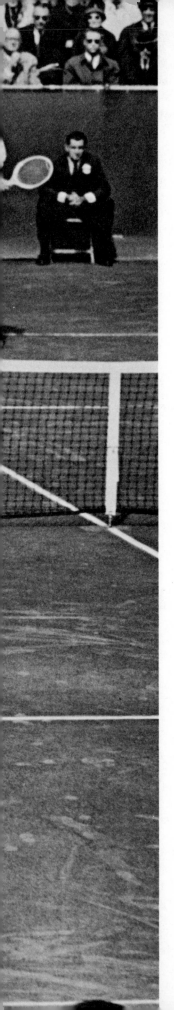

The most important single stroke in the game is the service, and the second most important is the return-of-serve. A player with a weak delivery is at a disadvantage every time he starts a game; a player with a poor return-of-service must have a really fine delivery to overcome the great handicap of weak groundstrokes. The well-rounded player has a good delivery and a reliable, perhaps aggressive, return-of-serve; the champion has a superb service and an extremely accurate, forceful return.

THE BEGINNER

The main objective for the beginner in hitting his return-of-serve is to get the ball in the court. He should not be concerned about low clearance over the net, depth, pace or placement. His goal is to *get the ball in*. Not until he learns to return consistently should he attempt to acquire depth, accuracy or speed.

BEGINNER'S FOREHAND POSITION

When the beginner receives in the forehand court, he stands on the baseline, three to four feet inside his forehand alley line. If his opponent is serving weakly, he can move inside the baseline by one or two steps; if his opponent's service is strong, he can step back two or three feet behind the baseline. He stands in the ready position, with knees flexed, feet apart, racket held in front of him and weight on the balls of his feet. He is in a position to turn his shoulders quickly right or left, and the fingers of his left hand cradle the racket throat so that he can easily shift from forehand to backhand grip. As soon as the ball leaves his opponent's racket, he takes the correct grip and at the same time turns his shoulders to the side where the ball will be coming. He is ready to move forward into the ball or to hop back if he has misjudged it. Before the ball has come over the net, he has started his backswing. By the time the ball bounces, his side is to the net and both he and his racket are moving toward the ball. He takes a full stroke, the emphasis being on lifting the ball well above the net so that it will go in the court.

BEGINNER'S BACKHAND POSITION

When the beginner returns service in the backhand court, his position is similar to the position he uses in the forehand court—he stands on or near the baseline, two to three feet to the right of his backhand alley line. His objective is not to hit either a down-the-line or a crosscourt but simply to get the ball into the court. The beginner must be able to hit just about every serve back into court before he attempts to make his shot more effective.

Steadiness is the making of a good tennis player. The man who hits four balls out and then knocks off a sizzling winner will invariably lose since his batting average is only 20%.

After you have acquired steadiness, you work on *depth*. Short balls give your opponent a chance to make a winner, whereas deep balls pin him on the baseline and prevent him from taking control of the play. Once you have learned depth, *accuracy* follows. The player then learns to hit the ball down the line or crosscourt. Only after you have acquired consistency, depth and accuracy can you add pace to your game. As a beginner, if you keep in mind the various stages through which you must progress, you will not try to hit a ball too hard until you have mastered the art of getting it into court with consistency, depth and placement.

THE INTERMEDIATE PLAYER

The intermediate player takes the return-of-serve exactly as the beginner, but he is more concerned about depth and accuracy. Intermediates seldom play against net-rushers, and therefore they need not be concerned with low net clearance. As long as one's opponent is in the backcourt, the ball can clear the net by 10 or 15 feet. The higher the ball goes over the net, the more likely it is to land deep; a low net-skimmer usually lands in the area of the service court, and therefore it is effective only against an opponent who is coming to net.

The intermediate player has learned to control the ball. He is trying to do a little more than simply get the ball back into the court area. He is not yet fully proficient, but he can hit a ball deep to his opponent's backhand with reasonable consistency. The intermediate will win most of his points by hitting with better depth and consistency than his opponent.

As the player advances from the intermediate class into the realm of the tennis knowledgeable, he usually acquires one strong weapon. Generally it is his forehand. It can be quite good for an attack against the weak service of an opponent. If the service bounces short and high, the "intermediate-advanced" player can hit either a deep, forceful forehand down the line or a very sharp forehand crosscourt. If this is not an outright point winner, it comes close to being so, since it forces the opponent to hit an even weaker return.

As the intermediate-advanced player builds up his strength to the point where his forehand be-

comes a real threat, he will frequently run arou[nd] a service directed to his backhand to take it on h[is] more powerful forehand.

THE ADVANCED PLAYER

The advanced player has a much larger repertoi[re] of shots. He is capable of playing against a serv[er] who takes the net because his return-of-serve is lo[w] hard and accurate. He is extremely aggressi[ve] against a weak server, and he can vary forcing [re]turns with drop shots. The beginner returns hi[gh] the intermediate with depth, the intermedia[te] advanced with accuracy and some speed, and t[he] advanced player with speed and variety.

The advanced player is not only a master of [all] the shots but also a strategist. He plays his o[wn] strength but he also plays his opponent's wea[k]nesses. He learns to block a hard service, to ch[ip] and come in against a soft hitter, to hit aggressive[ly] against a slow-footed player, to use spin to break [up] an opponent's rhythm, to drop shot against a ba[se]liner, and to use dipping balls, lobs and occasio[nal] bullets against net rushers.

RIPOSTES TO SERVES

The intermediate player will have troub[le] handling a wide-breaking slice, a deep and hi[gh] bouncing American twist and a cannonball. Ev[en] the advanced player will occasionally have difficu[lty] with these serves. The wide slice to the foreha[nd] pulls the player to his right; the bounce is low a[nd] the ball has a forward motion: The correct ripo[ste] to a very wide slice serve to the forehand in t[he] forehand court is a ball deep to the center or a hi[gh] lob, so the receiver can get back into position; [a] net-skimming forehand down the line against a n[et]-rushing server; or, far less frequently, a very sha[rp] forehand crosscourt which has almost no saf[e] margin.

The American twist is usually placed to the [re]ceiver's backhand. It bounces high and spins to t[he] left. The receiver must therefore hit a high ba[ck]hand return-of-serve, which is difficult against [a] net-rushing server. The receiver attempts to hit t[he] serve before it bounces too high and too wide. [He] therefore *steps in* on the American twist, which h[as] a great deal of hop but not much speed. The corr[ect] riposte is a backhand down the line against a n[et] rusher, a backhand crosscourt against the ra[re] American twist server who stays in the backcou[rt,] a low, dipping return or a lob. (Lobs, of course, a[re] always directed to the opponent's backhand.)

Very few players can drive-return a cannonb[all] service. Most prefer to block it, since there is n[ot] enough time to take a backswing and still meet t[he] ball in front of the body. The block return-of-ser[ve] should be low against the net-rusher and de[ep] against the server who stays in the backcourt. T[he] ceiver has so little time that he must see the ball leave his opponent's racket and make his movement immediately. If he delays at all, the ball will be moving his racket rather than the racket moving the ball. The cannonball is so forceful that blocking and lobbing are recommended in preference to a drive return-of-serve.

THE DOUBLES RETURN-OF-SERVE

There are four kinds of returns-of-serve in doubles and they are effective only if they go into court and if they are properly disguised. The lob over the server's partner is a perfect return-of-service—unless the server's partner has seen the lob coming. This is true also of the other three returns —the hard, low crosscourt; the soft, dipping ball; and the acute angle.

The beginner is not yet ready to play doubles against a net-rushing server. When a beginner plays doubles against players of his own caliber, it is like four people playing singles on a doubles court. The intermediate, however, has acquired a low return-of-service and he can therefore alternate this return with a lob over the server's partner. The advanced player can lob, dink and drive.

There is a fifth return-of-serve which is used against a "poacher" (one who frequently crosses to cut off the receiver's return). You must hit down the alley occasionally to keep him "honest." But unless this shot is disguised (and hit with pace), it is simply a set-up for the opponent. Otherwise you lob over the server's partner or hit crosscourt to the incoming server. The basis of the doubles return-of-serve is, therefore, the crosscourt, which is varied occasionally with lobs and with a hard down-the-line to the poaching net-man.

The best doubles players are those who hit the best returns-of-serve. Doubles play is primarily based on a net game, but a reliable, varied return-of-serve is almost as important. It is the return-of-serve rather than the volley that causes the server to lose his delivery game.

SUMMARY

Many players will spend a half-hour hitting forehands or backhands and another half-hour practicing volleys and overheads. The return-of-serve—the second most important shot in the game—is neglected. You can only practice return-of-serve one way—by playing. Only through practice sets will you acquire the accuracy, consistency, pace and variety required of a good player.

McKinley is drawn wide on a forehand return-of-serve on grass, and he is taking a full stroke with topspin. He has had time to bring his left foot in front of his right, closing his stance, as well as to make a full swing so that the serve cannot have been too hard. It it were, Chuck would lunge with open stance and preferably block the ball.

CHAPTER 16

The Singles Game

Tennis is a fascinating game because there is endless variety of plays. You can be a cat-and-mou player, a slugger, a steady player, a serve-and-n rusher, a trick artist, or a "chess player," dependi upon your personality and your skill. Each play will eventually find the game for which he is b suited, although he will occasionally shift to a other style simply for the fun of trying a ne technique. The pleasures of the game include lear ing variations and trying new approaches. One the most enjoyable facets of the sport is trying o a new technique against a player who will susceptible to it.

FOR THE BEGINNER

Only at the beginning stage is the player limit in variety. The novice must acquire sound stro before he learns variations, and he must al achieve steadiness before learning accuracy, spin a pace. In the beginning stages, therefore, the learn gives his full attention to executing the strokes c rectly. As he begins to play sets, the emphasis is st on proper stroking and, gradually, on getting t ball into court with regularity.

The beginner should not play a practice set un he has first learned to get his serve into court. If is serving one or two double-faults a game, it is more profitable for him to spend an hour practici his serve. He should never expect to win his pra tice sets. However, he will learn a lot from each he plays and within a short time he will be winni points and perhaps games from players a lit better than he.

The beginner's only object is to get the ball ir court. His groundstrokes should clear the net by or 15 feet, his first serve should go into cou regularly and he should make as few errors as p sible. He never tries for a winner. His concentrati is on the ready position, footwork, stepping into t ball, executing a full stroke and getting back position immediately. He never tries to hit the b hard. His object is to sustain a rally as long as p sible. He tries to watch the ball leave his opponen racket so that he can get set for the next shot.

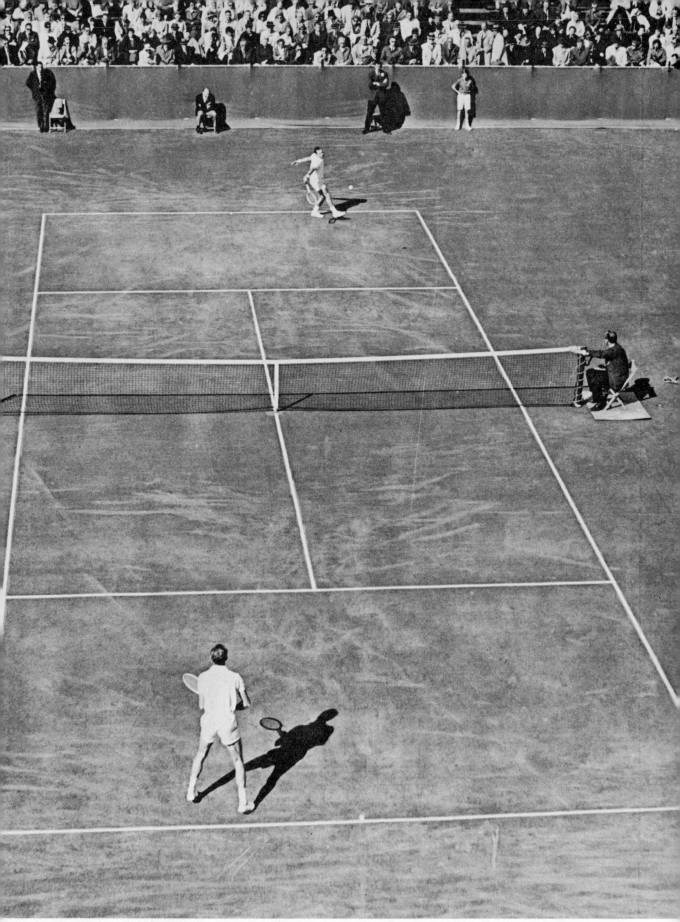

e acme of tennis is the Davis Cup Challenge Round, here played in Cleveland. Fred Stolle has served in
e left court and has resumed the ready position, while Chuck McKinley slices a backhand down the line.
rves are as important a factor as strokes in Davis Cup play. and McKinley had the edge on a nervous Stolle,

THE INTERMEDIATE

The intermediate player should not be content simply to get his first service into court. He need not try to serve hard but he should learn placement and depth. All his serves should be hit to the receiver's backhand. If he can spend an hour a week practicing his serve, he will soon be able to hit his delivery regularly to the backhand. The intermediate is not concerned with skimming the net but with getting the ball into court with great depth and with a certain amount of accuracy. The beginner is content to hit the ball into the court, whether or not it falls short; the intermediate must get the ball past the service line and can count himself successful if most of his shots land within two feet of the baseline. The beginner has no plan when he plays; the intermediate does have an elementary plan which involves playing his opponent's backhand or hitting deep, consistent crosscourts. The intermediate can also attempt to put away any short, high ball by stepping in and stroking it deep to a corner. He only forces on a short ball.

The intermediate-advanced player is developing a strength. He works on acquiring a slice on his service. He forces when his opponent serves short and high. He hits all short balls hard and he follows up by going to net. He works on adding pace to his game by hitting the ball much farther in front of him than the intermediate player. He tries to maneuver his opponent by catching him moving the wrong way, by running him wide and by bringing him to net. He does not attempt to hit every shot hard, but he never babies a set-up (a short, high ball).

THE ADVANCED PLAYER

The advanced player should have a forceful serve and should be able to follow it to net on a fast court. He is developing a style of his own, finding out his strengths and his opponent's weaknesses. He may be primarily a hitter or primarily a steady player, but his footwork is far better than the intermediate's and he is now covering court very well. He is getting the feel of when to hit and when to retrieve, of when to come to net and when to stay back, when to hit crosscourt and when down the line, of when to play cautiously and when to go for the big one.

The advanced player never tries a shot he does not know. An axiom of winning tennis is: *hit those shots which will win you the most points*. This is called *percentage tennis*.

Few players consider the number of errors they make on a particular shot and the number of points they would make if they played the shot differently. If you are losing more than 50% of the points on a particular shot, you can draw one of the following

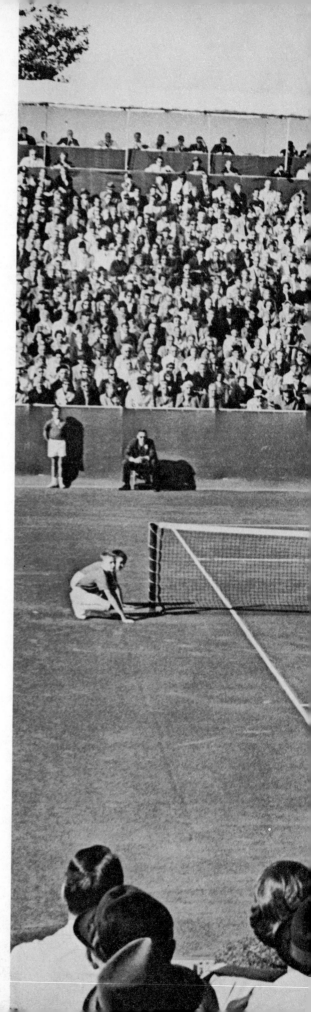

Roy Emerson, supremely confident, attacks on every serve, even on second balls on clay. He has taken his second step in and will now change direction, if necessary, while Dennis Ralston has to jump to his right to reach the serve down the middle. This is another scene from the Davis Cup Challenge Round.

conclusions: 1) your opponent is better than you; 2) the shot may be effective against a lesser player but it is not effective against a better one; 3) you are not executing the shot properly; 4) you are executing the shot at the improper moment; 5) it is a shot more suitable to doubles than to singles; 6) it is a shot more effective against a baseliner than a net-man; 7) the shot is falling too short, setting up too high, or going to your opponent's strength.

In singles play, you are not only trying to maneuver your opponent; he is also trying to maneuver you. If he pulls you wide to your forehand and you return wide to his forehand, you have left your whole backhand court open. When you run wide on either forehand or backhand the proper return is a deep ball to the center, a lob or an outright winner. If you try only the outright winner, you will undoubtedly lose more than 50% of the points. To play *percentage tennis*, you must, like a billiards player, understand the shape of the court and the safe and unsafe angles. Some of them are listed below.

SAFE SHOTS IN PERCENTAGE TENNIS

1. *Serve every ball deep to the backhand.* The wide ball to the forehand is extremely dangerous unless it is used to catch the opponent by surprise. Even if the opponent's backhand is stronger, his forehand return-of-serve is usually more forceful and deeper.

2. *Your regular return-of-serve in the forehand court should be deep to the backhand.* The only time you hit a forehand crosscourt is when you can hit forcefully enough to put the opponent in trouble or to make an outright winner.

3. When receiving serve in the backhand court, *hit your backhand down the line against a net-rushing server or deep to your opponent's backhand if he chooses to stay back.* If you hit the crosscourt on the net-rusher, it is easier for him to cut it off; if you hit the down-the-line against a server who is staying back, you will probably not get as mu depth and you will open up the court on your fo hand side to his forehand crosscourt.

4. *Never try an ace on second serve.* There is far greater safety factor in a slice and no one c afford a double-fault.

5. *Try your drop shots early in the match* eith for outright winners or to tire the opponent. Nev try them toward the closing stages since this is t time the opponent will go all out to get to the ba

6. *When you get a short forehand and want follow it to net, always hit it down the line to t opponent's backhand.* Hit crosscourt only for t outright winner but not as the approach shot.

7. *When you come to net on a forehand dow the-line, stand to the right of the center service l* so that you can cut off the backhand down-the-li He has to have a great backhand crosscourt shot pass you.

8. *When coming in on your backhand to t opponent's forehand, play to the left of the cen service line.* This enables you to cover the dow the-line and all but the sharpest crosscourt.

9. *When you are down 30-40, always get yo first serve in.* Use more spin and less pace to be su it goes into court.

10. *When you are pulled wide and your opp nent is at net, the safest shot is a high defens lob.* It is almost impossible for you to hit an o right winner, and any other shot will be a set-up the opponent. The lob will at least get you ba into the point again.

11. *Play the surface.* Take the offensive and harder on a fast surface. Don't follow your se to net on a slow surface. Catch your oppone moving in the wrong direction on a slippe surface.

These axioms of *percentage tennis* will help y by giving you a feel for the right and the wro shots. Practice will be more enjoyable when t "foolish" strokes are left out of your repertoi

Alex Olmedo (facing page) is serving in the Forest Hills Stadium. He tosses to the right of his body. His a is straight on the toss, his knees are bent, and the racket head is just about to come down behind his ba

CHAPTER 17

The Doubles Game

Barry MacKay serving in the right court is on his way in to net li[ke] every good player in doubles. Hugh Stewart, his partner, is in prop[er] ready position for aggressive men's doubles. He stands halfway betwee[n] the center service line and the singles sideline, about six feet fro[m] the net, ready to poach over to the center line or beyond to cut o[ff] any but a wide, low return. Stewart, like all good doubles players, is qui[te] willing to chance being passed down his alley occasionally, and eve[n] being lobbed over—although this happens infrequently because of h[is] fast reflexes and long reach.

In doubles, the two most important single strokes
are the volley and the return-of-serve. The big
serve counts for a little less than in singles, and
most players prefer the slice or twist which will
cause the opponent to hit up and which will enable
the server to get into a good volleying position.
The server and his partner have the advantage, and
between them they attempt to dominate from the
net. The volleyers have the edge over the ground-
strokers and, except in intermediate tennis, one
almost never hears of a team that does not volley
winning a big tournament.

A few great doubles players have had big
cannonball serves; most of them have had fine slices
or American twists. A few great doubles players
have had crushing groundstroke returns-of-serve;
most of them relied on pace mixed with lobs and
touch shots. A good doubles player has a reliable
serve, great reflexes at net, an accurate and consistent overhead, a fine and well-disguised return-of-
serve and aggressiveness in poaching. He hits all his
groundstrokes low but not necessarily hard, and
when he is at net and gets an opening, that is the
end of the point.

Doubles is a team game. An aggressive player and
a touch artist can successfully team together, the
latter setting up the former. One player may be a
safety volleyer who can consistently hit deep volleys
down the center; the other may be an aggressive
poacher who will take chances to end the point
immediately. Two different tennis personalities can
blend beautifully as a team, with one providing the
consistency and the other the aggressiveness.

WHY THE POOR PLAYER FAILS

The bad doubles player fails to get his first serve
to court with any regularity, errs frequently on
first volleys, telegraphs his lobs, tries to hit every
return-of-serve hard, does not keep the ball low, gets
caught behind the service line in his first volley,
never poaches or else poaches but does not put the
ball away, lobs too seldom, fails to keep an aggressive opponent "honest" by hitting an occasional
ball down his alley, plays too close to the service
line or too much on top of the net or, worst of all,
tells his partner what he did wrong.

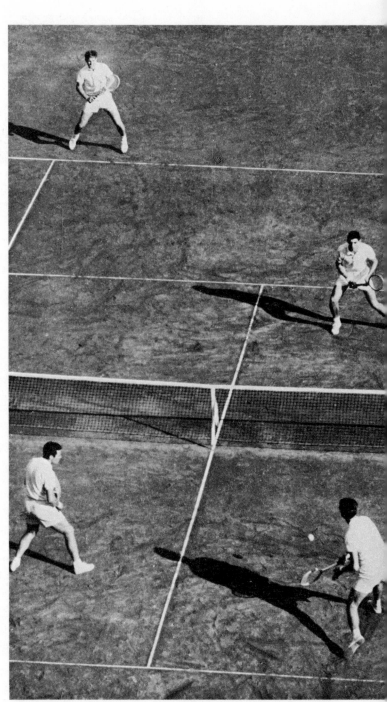

This is classic doubles play on the volley off return-of-
serve in the right court. The most striking feature is the
alertness of all the players: Hugh Stewart, who has just
returned serve from behind the baseline (unusual in top
doubles); his partner Barry MacKay, who is eager to
poach if the opponent's volley is too close to the center;
Orlando Sirola, who is well in for his first volley; and
Nicola Pietrangeli, Sirola's partner, who is following the
ball in good ready position.

WHAT IT TAKES

Concentration and alertness are extremely important in doubles, since most of the play is from the net. There is less time to be prepared and the play is very fast. The serving team is the aggressor, boring in and attempting to solicit high returns. The receiving team is the defender, keeping the ball low and trying whenever possible to take the net away from their opponents.

The novice is likely to waste everybody's time trying to play doubles. The intermediate will find that the doubles game will improve his singles, although it will be some time before he can follow his serve to net with any efficiency. Still, he will learn disguise, how to put away a high volley, how to run back for an overhead, the importance of the first serve and the value of the lob. The intermediate should not poach—he is not yet proficient in the volley—and should cover only his own area of the court. The advanced player can poach providing his batting average is at least 50% on outright winners.

Dennis Ralston (nearest camera) always starts his return of serve on the baseline, then moves forward a step, then lunges at the ball. Roy Emerson has hit to Ralston's forehand; this is Dennis' way of cutting down the angle—he moves forward. Ralston's partner, Chuck McKinley, is ready to move to center to intercept Emerson's first volley.

When in doubt, hit down the middle in doubles. Both Ralston and McKinley have moved to cover the sho
and while Ralston (left) is closer to the middle, McKinley will hit it because he is closer to the net and has
big jump-reach for the poach on his forehand side.

in the play is down the middle, with all four players net. The advantage is with Alex Olmedo (left front) has a high ball to drive-volley between Giam- lva (left rear) and MacKay.

Giammalva (left rear) and Seixas will surely lose this point. Someone has tried to lob over Rosewall, but he reached the ball and has a perfect opening. His partner is Hoad.

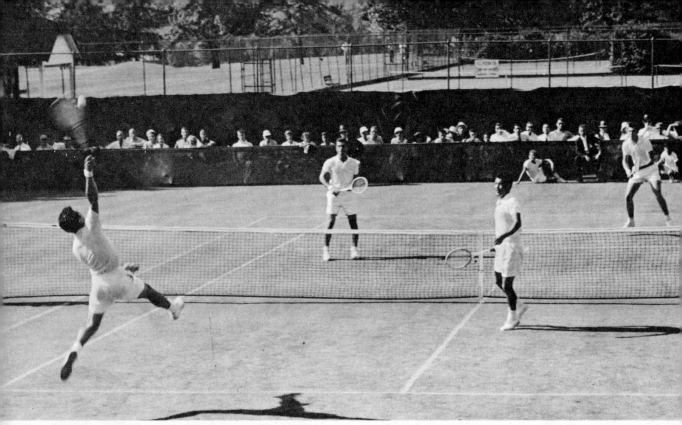

This lob over the head of Pancho Contreras is good enough so that Giammalva and MacKay (back court) ha a chance for the point, unless Contreras hits a great overhead. His partner, Mario Llamas, stays quite clo in, but Giammalva and MacKay can take the offensive here. The scene is a tie between U.S. and Mexico.

Bob Hewitt and Fred Stolle (near court), a great team, here play Roy Emerson (far left) and Neale Fraser a Wimbledon. All four Austrialians are top doubles players and all four here are at net, although Stolle and He witt are in closer. They have the edge, with Hewitt hitting down on a stroke-volley barely above net level.

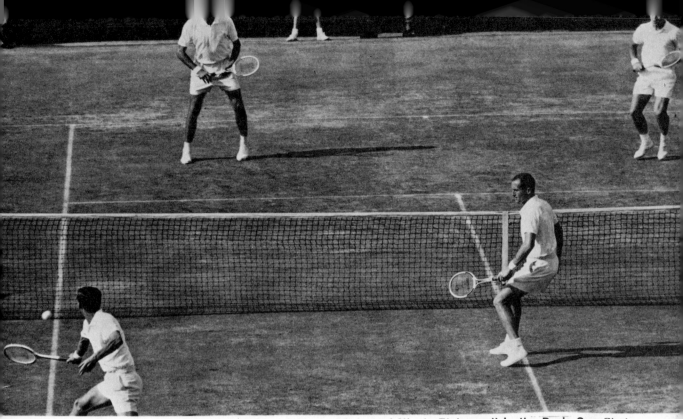

ere Emerson (near left) and Fraser are playing Orlando Sirola and Nicola Pietrangeli in the Davis Cup Chal-
nge Round in Australia. The Italians were a fine team, but Sirola is not standing in here on Pietrangeli's
rvice return, which Fraser has not intercepted (see how far he moved over) and Emerson is volleying.

ere is another sample of classical Australian doubles, played at Wimbledon. The only time Fraser (far court,
ght) will be on the baseline will be when he is returning serve and the serve was so good he could not come
 on the return, which is probably what happened here, or if he is lobbed over and must run back.

CHAPTER 18

Tips For

The Advanced Player

When an advanced player is working on a stro[ke]
or trying to change his style of play, the m[ost]
suitable opponent is a player whom he can b[eat]
without being extended. If he plays someone w[ho]
is his equal or who is better, he will find hims[elf]
pressed on his strokes or unable to accomplish [the]
change he is contemplating.

There should be no pressure on a player wh[en]
he is changing his game, and it is therefore not f[air]
to himself to try something new against a stro[ng]
opponent. If he is changing his style or his strate[gy]
his best opponent is a steady one who does not fo[rce]
too much but who gets enough balls back to ma[ke]
the practice interesting.

Many a player whose game is "off" will find th[at]
he can get back into the groove by playing someo[ne]
against whom he has unlimited confidence. Agai[nst]
a lesser player one can try a net attack or a mo[re]
offensive style of baseline play or a more aggressi[ve]
serve.

Play against a variety of games—against s[pin]
artists, touch players, sluggers, retrievers, tacticia[ns,]
strokeless wonders. Each type of opponent provi[des]
a different challenge. You can develop an asso[rt]-
ment of ripostes against chop artists, big serve[rs,]
net-rushers, dinkers, lefties and players with [big]
forehands or undercut backhands or heavy topspi[n.]

There is value in playing opponents who [are]
worse and opponents who are better. If you wa[nt]
to improve you should not play either catego[ry]
exclusively. Against a lesser player you can expe[ri]-
ment with spins, drop shots, a net attack or baseli[ne]
play. Against a better opponent there is always [the]
danger of overhitting or of pressing, but playi[ng]
against superior competition can make you mo[re]

ert, faster, better grooved and more conscious of
ur weaknesses.

IMPROVING YOUR GAME

What factors will make you a better player?
* Developing your strokes and practicing them
gularly
* Understanding the angles of the court
* Knowing your own weaknesses and recognizing
ur strengths
* Watching top players and analyzing their games
* Playing a variety of opponents
* Working on your doubles as well as your singles
* Perfecting the basics of the game—the serve,
e overhead, the volley, forehand, backhand, half-
lley, drop shot and lob.

There is a certain amount of self-analysis re-
uired in improving. If you have had a bad day,
you know why? Perhaps you were pushing the
ll instead of stroking it, moving back from your
lleys instead of hitting them, babying your serve
overhitting it, taking the ball behind you instead
in front of you, trying for outright winners in-
ead of working the point, resting on your heels
stead of bouncing on your toes, moving away
m instead of into the ball, getting flustered in-
ead of keeping cool, hitting to your opponent's
ength instead of to his weakness, tossing the ball
far behind you instead of to the side of you,
winding up too late or too early.

If you have a tendency to grip your racket too
sely or to keep your knees too straight or to let
e ball drop or to play too far back, keep a check
t and refer to it occasionally. Make sure you have
t reverted to old errors.

If you are having a particularly bad week or

month, go back to the fundamentals. Review the
ready position, check your balance and your swing,
slow down your strokes so that you can analyze
them yourself. Possibly ten minutes on the backboard will get you back in the groove. If you have
been undercutting your backhand or hitting your
forehand too flat, concentrate on putting topspin
on the ball. If you have been netting your volleys,
try to hit them deep. If you have been spraying the
fences with your overheads, cut down on your pace
and think only of accuracy. In each case, go over
the steps of the stroke one by one to see if you have
neglected some important aspect.

Work out a strategy before a match, but once
you step on the court the strokes must be automatic.
Your strategy should be changed if you are losing;
it should not be varied if you are winning. On the
odd games, as you change sides, try to figure out
where you are losing your points and where you
are winning them. Perhaps you are not lobbing
enough or perhaps too much. It may be that you
are allowing the opponent's serve to break away
from you instead of stepping in to hit it before
the spin carries it away. Perhaps you are not prepared for the opponent's change of pace and are
caught by his occasional drop shots or spins. Both
your mind and your eyes must be alert—you are
not simply playing a ball; you are playing an opponent.

If you practice, if you think, if you analyze, if
you work with heart and eagerness, your game will
steadily improve. Your serve will be bigger, your
court coverage better, your reaction time will
quicken and you will get ever more pleasure out of
the game.

glossary

ace: a service that cannot be returned by the opponent.

ad: after the players have each won three points in the same game, the next point is called "advantage" or "ad" for the player who has won it.

alley: the area of the court bounded by the singles sideline and the doubles sideline. It is used only in doubles after service has been put into play.

American twist: a type of service in which the racket moves across the ball in a rightward direction rather than through the ball in a forward direction.

angle game: a style of play in which the angles of the court are used. Specifically, it refers to the short angles, *e.g.,* the player hits a forehand crosscourt which lands inside his opponent's service line and close to the opponent's forehand sideline.

approach shot: a shot hit by a player as he is moving toward net.

backswing: the wind-up of a stroke before racket and ball make contact.

"big game": a style of play in which the emphasis is on a big service and a net attack.

big server: a man with a powerful service.

block: the return of a ball by holding the racket stiffly in front of the body; there is neither backswing nor follow-through. It is used almost exclusively against a big service.

bullet: a hard-hit ball.

cannonball: a hard-hit service.

chip: a chop which is used either to return serve or as an approach shot.

chop: an undercut stroke which is hit in front of the body. It has only a small wind-up and follow-through.

crosscourt: a ball which is hit from one side of the court to the diagonally opposite side.

delivery: a service.

deuce: the score as announced when each player has won three points each, four points each, five points, etc. in the same game.

die: descriptive of a ball that scarcely bounces at all.

dink: a soft shot without pronounced spin wh drops just as it comes over the net. It is used force a net player into error or to make him high.

dipping balls: balls that barely clear the net, th drop fast and short.

double-fault: two consecutive errors on the sa service point, which cause the server to lose point.

down-the-line: a ball which is hit from one po in the court to the point directly opposite, e a forehand down-the-line that goes to the op nent's backhand.

drive: a forehand or backhand groundstroke.

drive volley: a volley in which a groundstro wind-up is taken.

drop shot: a ball hit with so much underspin t it drops immediately after it clears the net, th bounces with little or no forward motion "dies").

drop volley: a volley hit with so much undersp that it bounces like a drop shot.

error: any ball that hits the net or the area o side the court boundaries. The player who co mits the error loses the point.

fault: an error on first service. The player d not lose the point but is allowed another serv without penalty.

fifteen: the first point that a player wins in a p ticular game.

flat serve: a service without any spin.

flat shot: a groundstroke without any spin.

follow-through: the motion of arm and rac after the ball has been hit.

forced error: an error made by a player becau of a good shot on the part of his opponent.

forcing shot: a shot hit by a player which p duces either an outright error or a weak retu

game score: points are reckoned as "15," "3 "40" and "*game*" rather than "1," "2," "3" a "4". A player must win a game by at least t points. Therefore, if each player has th points, the score is called "*deuce*" rather th "40-40" or "40-all." The player who wins

xt point has *"advantage"* (not "50-40"). If he
es the next point, the score goes back to deuce.

ooved": descriptive of a player who knows his
okes or tactics so well that he does not have
think about them and performs them auto-
tically.

oved stroke: a stroke with which the player
so familiar that he performs it automatically.

undstroke: a stroke hit after the ball has
unced more than 8" or 12" high.

f-volley: a shortened stroke hit immediately
er the ball has bounced and before it has risen
a height of 8" or 12".

ting deep: hitting to an area on or within two
three feet of the baseline.

ting short: hitting into an area in the vicinity
the service line.

a ball which ticks the net on the serve but
ds in the proper area; the point is replayed.
ditionally: the replaying of a point because of
side interference.

a ball that will rise over the head of an op-
nent standing at net.

e: zero (no points or no games) in scoring.

cord: any ball that hits the net other than on
vice. If the ball lands within the court boun-
ies, whether or not it ticks the net, it is good
l is in play.

man: a player whose position is inside the
vice line.

n racket face: the strings of the racket are al-
st parallel (rather than perpendicular) to the
und.

rhead: a stroke that is hit directly over the
d, normally with the arm fully extended.

-ball delivery: a soft service.

cement: a shot that is an outright winner that
not be touched by the opponent.

cher: net man in doubles who invades his
tner's area of the court in order to put away
olley.

y: hitting the ball back and forth across the
after the ball has bounced.

eiver: the man who is receiving serve.

erse twist: a rarely seen service in which the
ket moves across the ball in a leftward direc-
.

score: in tennis a player must win at least six
nes to take the set. However, he must have
more games than his opponent. He can win
set by 6-1, 6-2, 6-3, 6-4, 7-5, 8-6, 9-7, etc.

set-up: an easy shot, usually a short, high ball,
which a competent player can hit away for an
outright winner.

slice serve: a serve in which the racket comes
across the ball sideways and forwards at the
same time.

smash: an overhead.

sidespin: a kind of spin produced by pulling the
racket forward and toward the body as it contacts the ball.

spin: a method of hitting which produces a roll-
ing of the ball in the air either sideways (sidespin), forwards (overspin or topspin) or backwards (underspin).

thirty: the second point that a player gets in a
particular game.

topspin: a forward rotation of the ball after it has
been hit.

touch artist: a player who is a master of spins or
delicate shots.

touch shot: any shot that is produced by a delicate movement of the racket such as a drop shot,
a lob volley or an extremely angled shot.

twist: see American twist.

underspin: a backward rotation of the ball after
it has been hit.

volley: a ball that is hit before it bounces.

wide-breaking slice: a slice service with so much
spin that it pulls the receiver into or beyond the
alley.

TERMS THAT SHOULD NOT BE USED

"cut": one does not "cut" the ball; one can "drive"
it, "slice" it, "chip" it, "chop" it, "smash" it,
"underspin" it or "topspin" it.

"volley" for "rally": a volley is a ball that is hit
before it bounces; it is not a rally.

"smash a forehand": one can only smash an overhead; one can "hit a forehand hard," "powder
a forehand," "murder a forehand," "score a forehand placement" or "make a forehand winner."

"placement" for "ace": a service outright winner
(where the opponent does not touch the ball) is
an "ace;" all other outright winners (on groundstrokes or volleys or overheads) are "placements."

"six to two": one says "six-two" or "six-three"
(it is written 6-2 or 6-3).

"15 to 30": correct usage is "fifteen-thirty" (it is
written 15-30).

the **end**